FLYING HORSES, SECRET RIVERS,
MAGICAL CITIES

Anu Kumar is the author of more than 30 books for children. She has immersed herself in history for most of her life, having studied the subject in college and later at university. Besides writing for children, she also writes historical fiction for older readers, under the pseudonym Adity Kay. Her non-fiction articles are published regularly on Scroll.in. Anu lives in New Jersey, USA, with her family, and loves visiting museums and going on long hikes.

OTHER BOOKS BY ANU KUMAR

Her Name Was Freedom: 35 Fearless Women Who Fought for India's Independence (2022)

MythQuest Omnibuses (Four Volumes) (2021)

Wonder Kids: 100 Children Who Grew up to Be Champions of Change (2019)

Kings and Queens of India: Famous Rulers and Dynasties that Shaped the Country (2019)

Across the Seven Seas: Indian Travellers' Tales from the Past (2015)

Sarojini Naidu: The Nightingale and the Freedom Fighter (2014)

Swami Vivekananda: The Monk and the Reformer (2014)

Chanakya: The Kingmaker and the Philosopher (2013)

The Mahatma and the Monkeys (2009)

FLYING HORSES, SECRET RIVERS, MAGICAL CITIES

Incredible Adventures in India and Beyond

ANU KUMAR

hachette INDIA

First published in 2024 by Hachette India
(Registered name: Hachette Book Publishing India Pvt. Ltd)
An Hachette UK company
www.hachetteindia.com

1

ISBN 978-93-5731-597-5

Hachette Book Publishing India Pvt. Ltd
4th & 5th Floors, Corporate Centre
Plot No. 94, Sector 44, Gurugram – 122003, India

Typeset in Avenir Lt Std 11/15.2
by Manmohan Kumar, Delhi

FSC
www.fsc.org
MIX
Paper | Supporting responsible forestry
FSC® C010615

Printed and bound in India
by Thomson Press India Ltd.

To my sister, Soma –
remembering the years of quiet exploring in Odisha

CONTENTS

INTRODUCTION

TO BOLDLY GO WHERE NO ONE HAS GONE BEFORE

The 1800s were an amazing time. It was the age of discoveries and explorations, new knowledge and new freedoms. This period was somewhat different from the earlier explorations of the fifteenth century, that is, 600 years ago from now. These older journeys, such as those of Ferdinand Magellan, Vasco da Gama and Christopher Columbus, for instance, had been made to find new lands and new sea routes to India, and for conquest.

However, from the 1800s, explorations and journeys were made to gather knowledge. This was knowledge that empires needed to make themselves more secure and stronger, *and* knowledge that scholars and explorers pursued for the sake of it. Both purposes were linked, making this quest for knowledge quite a complicated enterprise. The reasons were many, and the actors involved were altogether a very interesting lot.

At the beginning of the eighteenth century, many believed they knew what the 'known world' looked like (though today, a phrase like this – 'known world' – is quite rightly contested): There were the kingdoms and monarchies across Europe, which saw themselves as 'modern', trying to set up their empires or colonies across Africa, Asia and parts of America too, which were considered 'backward' and 'mysterious' regions.

In Asia, the British were constantly competing against the French, the Danes, the Dutch as well as the Russians. This quest for territory came with a thirst for knowledge. To best your enemies, to get the upper hand, you had to have more information.

For this to happen, they needed experts, and there were many among them who were also interested in seeking knowledge for its own sake. To this category belonged the scientists, the explorers, the mountaineers, and the adventurers, who were passionate about seeking new lands, new places and new challenges. And they couldn't have done it alone.

Like-Minded Companions

There is more romance and less truth in stories about the lone traveller, journeying into the unknown, battling the odds and dangers. An adventurer always had help, and most times, this help, advice and support came from the locals, whose stories rarely appeared in the final accounts when these were written down. Explorers were also inspired by stories they had heard, including those of the researchers and explorers who had travelled before them. A quest for knowledge is nearly always a joint endeavour, an adventure in companionship, a mission based on shared wisdom and learning that is passed on.

For example, the first person you encounter as you turn the next few pages is William Moorcroft. He went on a search for the fastest horse imaginable. There were stories in myth about such horses, and there was an urgency about finding them as well. The British Indian army would be greatly helped by such animals. Moorcroft had the support of the government for a while, and help from merchants who loaned him goods to barter and negotiate his way through hostile territory. He also had his own small army – friends and associates (most of them Indian), his friend Mir Izzat Ullah and his helpers, along with the unnamed many who carried provisions, set up tents, cooked and guarded their camps.

Fitting In

There were Indians who did their own explorations too. Many had been doing this for centuries. These were people like Nain Singh Rawat and his cousin, Mani Singh, who lived in Kumaon in the Himalayan foothills. Their ancestors had made up the trading caravans to Tibet. This knowledge, their understanding of local ways, the region itself and the languages spoken there, proved helpful to the British surveyors who wanted to map the Himalayas.

Besides, the British wanted to know about the majestic Himalayas, and the forbidden land of Tibet, but also to have information about Russia, the giant empire to the north, and its motives.

Some of the locals accompanying the survey or exploration teams did indeed pen their stories in languages such as Persian, Bengali and Urdu. These were inaccessible for a long time, but then, many of them were also educated in English.

Mohan Lal 'Kashmiri', for example, worked as a Persian interpreter, for he knew English well too. He was a careful observer, noting even the smallest details. It was his knowledge of local ways and decision-making that helped save his life once in Kabul.

In the east, Sarat Chandra Das was inspired to make his own journeys when he read stories of other explorers, but his own travels were unique as well. Travelling to Tibet with his friend Lama Ugyen Gyatso, he was able to blend in easily, something a Britisher might not have been able to. As a scholar, Das was able to gain insights only a 'local' could.

Lasting Knowledge and Beauty

All these explorers risked a lot of danger in finding out new things, especially when many, like Ralph Izzard, felt that there was nothing left to explore anymore. But there were all these mysteries about flying horses, strange swamp creatures in the east, forbidden castles high in the mountains, secret magical plants deep in South America, a river's mysterious origins, the actual height of the very tall mountain peaks in the north, and so there were those who were driven to solve such mysteries, and who wouldn't rest till their questions had been answered.

In this process, they did provide the information that the administrators wanted, but they also richly contributed to the world's storehouse of knowledge. They broke many barriers in the process too – for instance, Fanny Workman was among the first women to address the Royal Geographic Society in the UK.

While some of them were avid explorers, others like the artist Colesworthy Grant, and Kinthup, a tailor by profession, serendipitously stumbled into such adventures. Some made friends, and others encountered the worst kind of rulers – bigots and cruel tyrants. Some were frustrated and yet left behind enduring stories, others discovered objects of beauty like Joseph Dalton Hooker's rhododendrons that found their way from the Himalayan foothills to aristocratic homes in England.

A thing of beauty, these explorers seem to tell us, takes a long search, and then lasts forever.

1

THE WORLD'S FASTEST HORSE

WILLIAM MOORCROFT'S JOURNEY

Chasing the swiftest horses took veterinary surgeon William Moorcroft very far – right into Tibet and Central Asia – and made him a legend! But did he find them, after all?

The Turkoman horse was a tall, fleet-footed stallion rumoured to roam freely in the steppes of Central Asia and the mountainous region in upper Tibet. Riding them, armies could cover distances at great speed, just like the fearsome Mongols had once done, several centuries ago. In the early nineteenth century, explorers, army men and adventurers from various countries set out in search of this elusive horse. They believed such horses would give a boost to their respective armies.

Some writers also called it the Yarkandi horse. A nineteenth-century British writer, Harriet Murray-Aynsley, wrote of the resemblance between horses in Scandinavia (northern Europe) and the Yarkandi horse. She cited a myth that it was the Scandinavian god Odin who got the horses from the Himalayas. In Nordic mythology, Odin himself rode an eight-legged winged horse called Sleipnir.

William Moorcroft was a veterinary surgeon who lived in India at a time when the British East India Company was establishing its control over large parts of the subcontinent. He was in charge of the East India Company's 'stud' – a place where horses were reared for the military – and he set off on an adventure to find this 'magical' horse. It gave Moorcroft more than he had bargained for. What he saw and wrote down in his journals revealed his curiosity and delight in finding out things, lost and old, that he himself had little idea of.

A Farm Boy Turned Surgeon

William Moorcroft was born in Ormskirk, a town in Lancashire, UK, in 1767. His grandfather, Richard Moorcroft, was interested in scientific techniques of farming (that is, farming that was aligned to seasons), and his grandmother, Dorothy, was a practical woman who was a hands-on farmer. His grandparents built their own house and devoted themselves to managing their extensive lands, and especially to dairy farming.

In 1747, Richard and Dorothy Moorcroft faced both desolation and joy. Their daughter, Ann, was born that year, but a cattle plague wiped out most of their dairy herd. Twenty years later, Ann's son William was born, and he grew up in his grandparents' house. He was deeply influenced by them.

Richard Moorcroft had a library of books and manuscripts that he later left to William. Meanwhile,

William decided to study surgery. For a long time, surgery was associated with barbers who carried out routine operations, but it was now becoming a respectable profession in its own right. William Moorcroft secured a prized surgical apprenticeship with the Liverpool surgeon, John Lyon.

While he was a pupil of Dr Lyon, the attention of all the physicians and surgeons of the Liverpool Infirmary was drawn to an illness that severely afflicted the horned cattle of a particular English district. It was feared that this illness would become an epidemic. Moorcroft, then a pupil, was sent to get a more hands-on experience, and it turned out to be a formative time. He decided to become a veterinary surgeon – one of the first of his times. As there was no veterinary school in London at the time, Moorcroft went to France and spent some time there.

THE NAME PLATE OUTSIDE WILLIAM MOORCROFT'S RESIDENCE AND CLINIC IN THE UK

Besides being a veterinary surgeon, William was a man of some unusual plans. He had ideas that were brilliant but difficult to implement, a pattern that would repeat itself for the rest of his life. He lost a lot of money in an unwise project to manufacture cast-iron horseshoes. These had the advantage of not rusting but turned out to be too heavy for horses and expensive to mass produce. When Moorcroft received an offer to go out to Bengal as Superintendent of the East India Company's military stud, he readily accepted. He left England in May 1808.

His job in Bengal was clearly defined. He was given the task of improving the poor breed of horses that made up the cavalry. As he wrote, at that time, the horses in his care were diseased and even undernourished. One of the first things he did was to introduce the cultivation of oats and make it a part of their daily fodder. Then, to permanently improve the state of the cavalry in India, Moorcroft passionately urged the introduction of the Turkoman horse, in preference to the Arab horse that, for a long time, had been imported from Arabia.

First, the Goats

In 1812, in search of the fabled horses, he set off on his first journey across the Himalayas. With a large caravan, he made his way to the plains between these mountains and the Kun Lun chain, close to the sources of the rivers Indus and Sutlej. He also rode up to the two lakes of Rakshastal and Mansarovar. Besides the natural difficulties of the way, he had to evade the vigilance of the Nepalese, who were, at that time, close to war with the British.

To add to his travails, the Chinese authorities also refused him permission to proceed via Tibet to Central Asia, so he could not move beyond the Himalayas. But he never gave up on his ideas. As he waited, he saw the potential of the goats native to this region, whose wool was used to make the shawls so popular back then. Moorcroft felt these goats could be bred in England. But this, like so many of his schemes, was doomed to failure.

He managed to get some goats out of Tibet, which were dispatched to England from 1813 onwards. The goats that survived the journey were sent to the estate of the Duke of Atholl in Scotland. But Scotland was not as cold as Tibet, or perhaps not high or dry enough either, to help the growth of the fine shawl wool. The animals were miserable. By October 1815, not a single male goat survived and only seven female ones remained. The wool that was produced proved of little value. Moorcroft attributed it to neglect and mismanagement. He remained convinced that had the goats been properly looked after, they could have produced commercial quantities of shawl wool outside Tibet.

On to a Fabled Land

Seven years later, he made his second journey to Central Asia again. He was desperate to enter the kingdoms here, to acquire the breed of horses he hoped to rear and domesticate in India. Moorcroft prepared carefully for the journey, and he set off again in 1819.

He had first sent, at his own expense, an intelligent friend, Mir Izzat Ullah, to map out the journey. Izzat

Ullah left Delhi in 1812 and proceeded to Kashmir, from where he went to Leh in Ladakh. Moving across Ladakh, he travelled to Yarkand in Central Asia, and by way of Kashgar, Khotan and Samarkand, he reached the fabled land of Bukhara, where large numbers of the famous Turkoman horse were rumoured to thrive. Mir Izzat Ullah came back to India via Balkh, Bamiyan and Kabul. This was the route Moorcroft hoped to take, for which he had to take the necessary permits from Ranjit Singh, the ruler of Punjab who then had control over Kashmir.

As Moorcroft set off for Bukhara, he negotiated and carried with him articles of merchandise that he thought would be in great demand in these regions. He took with him goods worth about 3,000 British pounds. Some of these he planned to sell or exchange in Kashmir for shawls. He also took with him about 2,000 pounds worth of coral and pearls. The proceeds of sales would go to buying horses. Indeed, he travelled with a great caravan of cottons, broadcloths made of wool, chintz, cutlery, and hardware, iron utensils, and tools provided by two Calcutta (now Kolkata) business houses with whom Moorcroft, at his persuasive best, had wrangled a deal.

Moorcroft set off from Bareilly towards the end of October 1819. In his company were his friend's son, George Trebeck, who was a draughtsman and surveyor; a medical officer Guthrie; his old assistant, Mir Izzat Ullah; and Ghulam Hyder Khan, a native of Bareilly, a 'stout soldier and faithful servant', as Moorcroft described him, and then there were helpers, porters, and several assistants. Moorcroft's party was really a small army, though it had peaceful intentions.

This entourage at one stage included six elephants and forty camels; at another, sixty porters, fourteen horses, four mules and a drove of bullocks; and at yet another, 300 porters! In addition, there were personal servants, grasscutters, grooms, a baker, a draughtsman and two botanical collectors. Moorcroft had about fifty people on his permanent payroll, and they all had to be fed, clothed and paid. Though he was generous, it was not always easy to retain men to help him. It proved impossible to find a blacksmith to accompany them, and some helpers deserted the expedition soon after the journey began, rather than take on the arduous mountain climb.

The North of the Country

In December 1819, they made a brief stop at Almora, and then at Joshimath. They waited so long for yaks and porters that by then the passes had closed. So Moorcroft decided to head to Srinagar and negotiate with Ranjit Singh, the king of Punjab, to head to Leh via Srinagar. His seeking to open negotiations with Ranjit Singh displeased the British, who were apprehensive of the king.

Srinagar was still recovering from the earthquake of September 1803 and the flooding that had followed some years later. More than half the city, Moorcroft noted, was in ruins. The palace, a spacious and ornamental structure, had been erected about three centuries ago, but being built of brittle stone, was now dilapidated and unoccupied.

What He Travelled With

Moorcroft certainly did not intend to travel rough. His blue accommodation tent, spreading over nine square feet and with high walls, came with Mirzapuri carpets, folding tables and chairs, a library of well over hundred reference books, and his portable, mahogany writing desk. His smaller sleeping tent was dominated by a splendid folding brass bedstead. This, when unpacked from its leather case and fully assembled with chintz hangings and mosquito netting, and with colourful bedside rugs, must have been quite a sight at the end of a long day.

Then there was the 'portable necessary house', a term first used by Garry Alder who wrote in 1985 about Moorcroft's Bukhara journey. This referred to portable bathrooms set up near the tents for the principal members of the party. Additionally, medicines were carried in a chest, along with catheters and other surgical instruments, weapons, ammunition, and cartridge boxes; surveying equipment, compasses, spyglasses, thermometers and barometer tubes; stationery; a collection of fishing lines; a vast array of other equipment including kaleidoscopes, silver and plated articles like teapots, soup tureens and sugar basins, telescopes, watches, cut-glass chandeliers, pistols, scissors and penknives.

The chief building, and one in resolute shape, was a *dharmshala*, an inn for travellers and pilgrims. Srinagar's bazaar, about a quarter of a mile in length, was broad and paved. The houses, mostly of stone, with slated and sloping roofs, were two storeys high. The lower storey usually served as a shop. The only goods manufactured were coarse linen and woollen cloths, mainly for domestic use.

He headed towards Lahore, which was Maharaja Ranjit Singh's capital, intending to seek his permission and help to move ahead towards Bukhara. As he headed westward from Srinagar, Ranjit Singh's chieftains and men stopped them. Petty chiefs bullied them, forcing them to part with some of their goods, or pay taxes.

The Gentle Doctor

Where he stopped, Moorcroft earned people's goodwill by setting up a temporary surgical practice. He dispensed his medical advice freely to all those who came to him.

At Hoshiarpur, despite a hostile chieftain, he devoted a considerable portion of his time to surgical practice and soon had many patients. The prevailing complaints were related to the eyes, and he operated on forty cases of cataract with fair success.

The operation was known to native practitioners and was usually performed by barbers, who doubled up as surgeons. Their instruments, however, were primitive and their methods could be clumsy. Moorcroft persuaded one of them to assist him, and also left

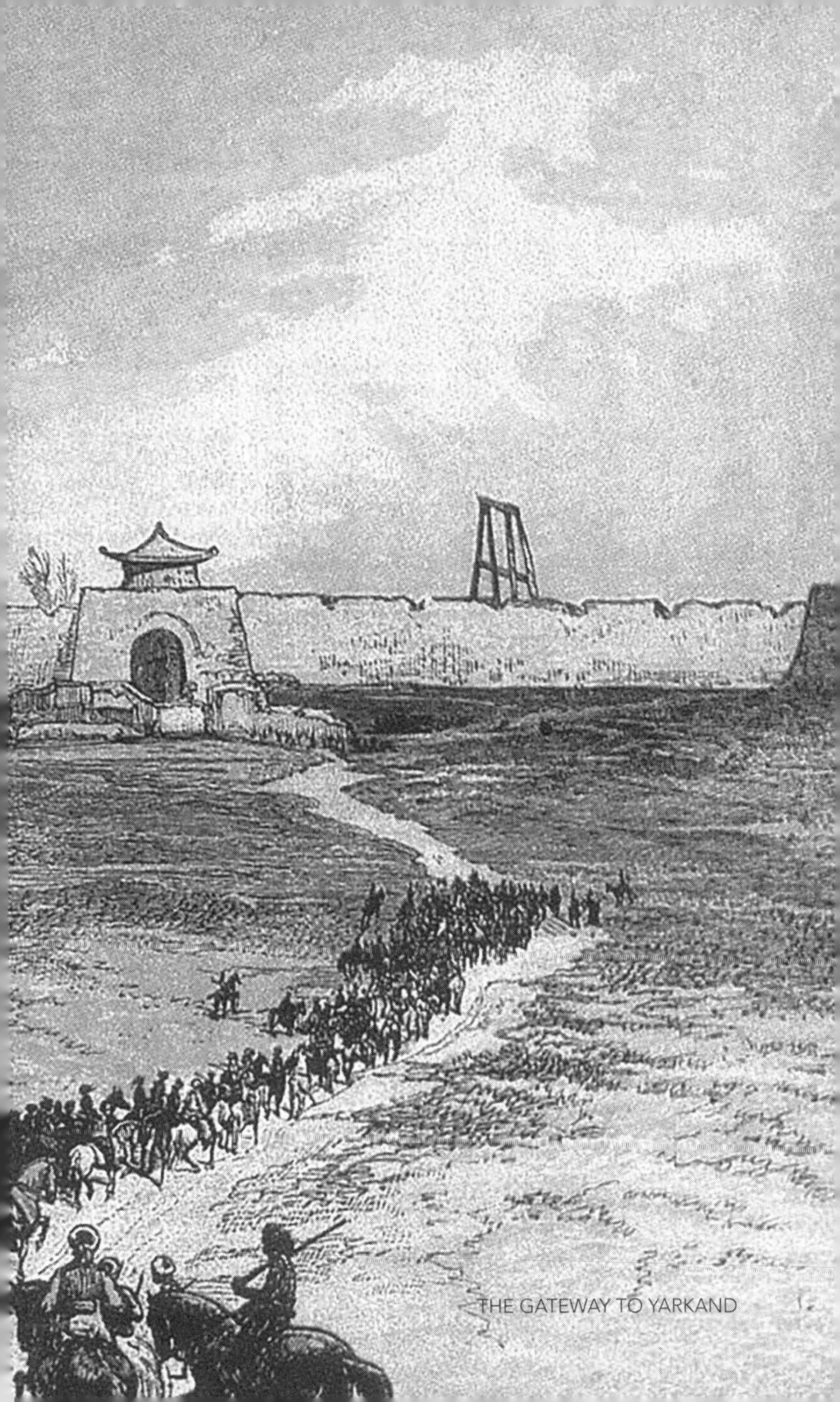

THE GATEWAY TO YARKAND

behind a set of his own instruments for the treatment of cataract.

In May 1820, when he reached Lahore, he headed for the Shalimar Gardens, commissioned by the Mughal emperor Shahjahan. He stayed in a chamber erected close to a well, with a reservoir nearby. The fountains helped cool his chamber considerably. Ranjit Singh had, to a great extent, beautified the gardens even more than before. The grounds were intersected by canals and neatly tiled walkways.

Gifts for Ranjit Singh

Ranjit Singh, known to be a generous host, first sent him sweet delicacies and money. Moorcroft refused the latter politely and diplomatically. Instead, he offered the king the few gifts he had brought. These included a pair of double-barrelled guns, a pair of triple-barrelled pistols, a sword, and the model of a cannon, complete with carriage and essential parts.

Ranjit Singh was greatly pleased with the pistols, and even more with the cannon. Knowing Moorcroft's interest, he ordered some of his own horses to be exhibited, and about fifty were mustered up for a review. They all had lavishly decorated bridles and saddles, and were of fine breeds – Arabian steeds, or those found in forest districts in the Punjab, while others were from Central Asia. The following morning, he saw the horses being exercised.

One of Ranjit Singh's pet themes was the state of his stud. Moorcroft was told that most of his horses were

A HORSE FROM MAHARAJA RANJIT SINGH'S STUD

presents from his tributary chieftains and *zamindar*s, and that the king often rewarded the donor of a superior animal with a village or a *jagir*. It was little wonder, Moorcroft recorded, that the king obtained the best horses for his own use.

Days in Ladakh

Moorcroft and his party reached Leh in September 1820. He would be stuck here for two years, until September 1822. Part of this delay was due to prolonged negotiations about heading to Yarkand, and the Chinese authorities in the end refused him entry. Another reason for the long wait in Ladakh lay in Moorcroft's financial difficulties. He had to gift away a lot to chieftains when passing through north India and Punjab. Now, unable to dispose of the

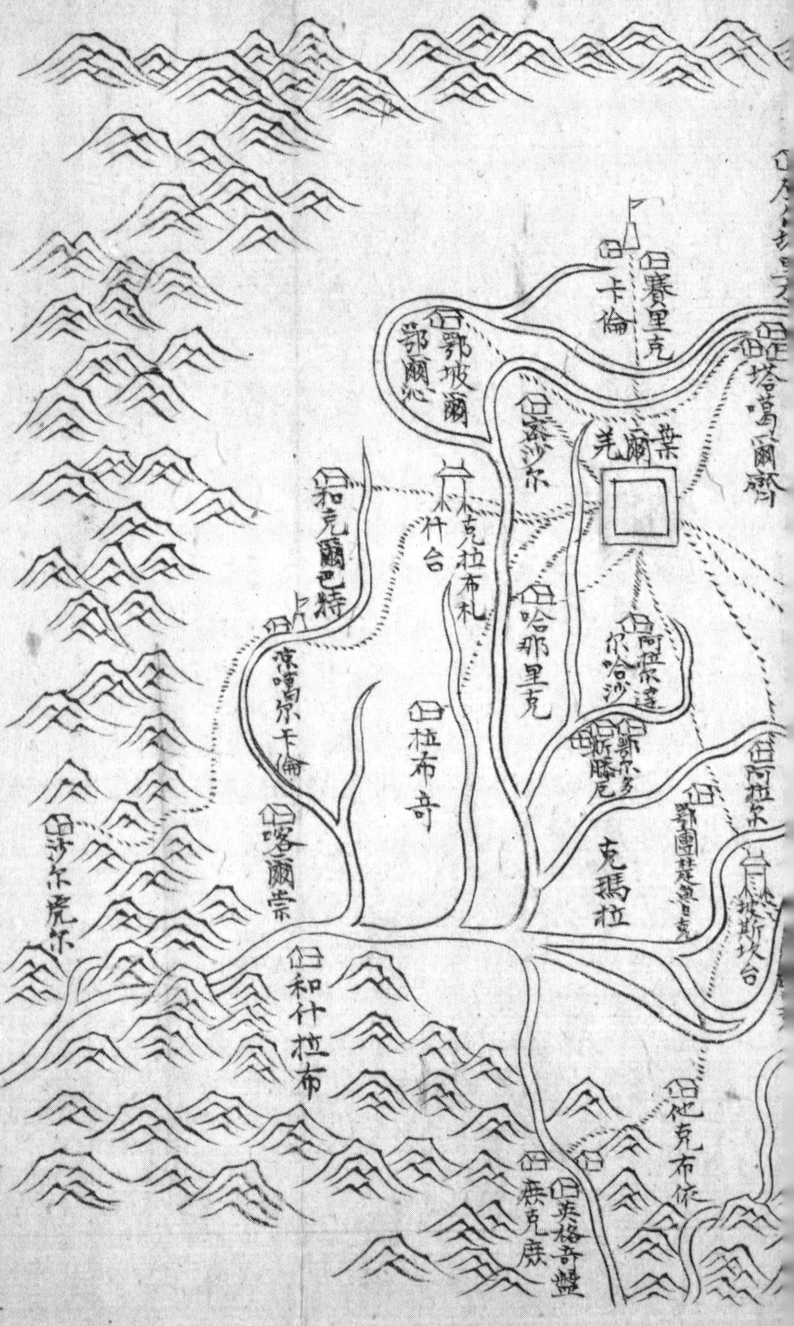

賽里克
卡倫
鄂坡爾
鄂爾沁
葉爾羌
塔噶爾齊
和克爾巴特
克拉布札
什台
哈那里克
拉布奇
喀爾崇
克瑪拉
阿拉爾
拔斯坎台
和什拉布
英格奇盤

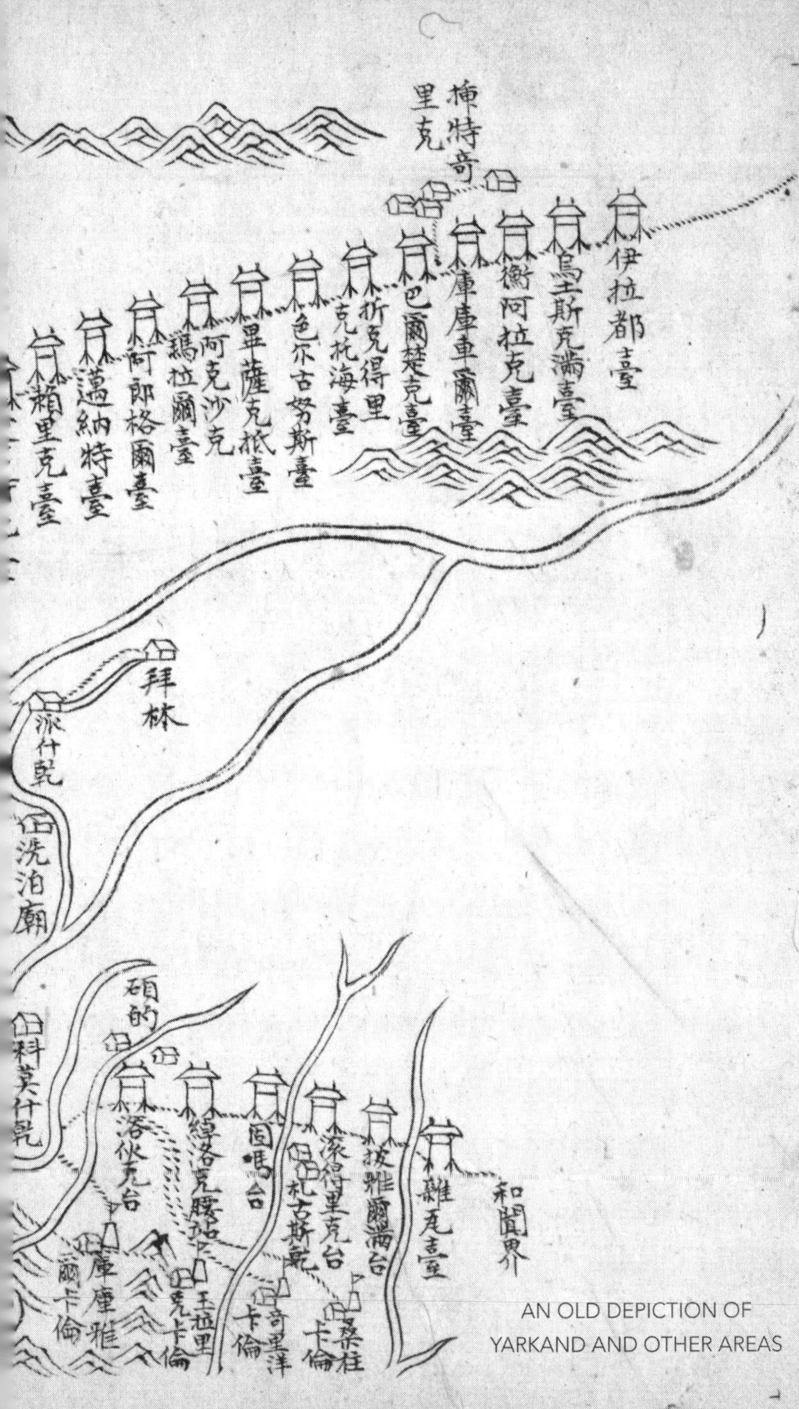

AN OLD DEPICTION OF YARKAND AND OTHER AREAS

remainder of the merchandise at a fair price, and the expense needed to maintain his party consisting of forty persons, Moorcroft's finances were under strain. He was obliged to seek credit from his agents in Calcutta, via the Resident at Delhi, Sir David Ochterlony.

The government of India, fed up with his overextended journey, soon refused to recognize Moorcroft in any diplomatic capacity, and once he was beyond the Punjab, he became pretty much a lone player.

Despite this, in Ladakh, he lost no time in opening his medical practice. He noticed there was a striking absence of illnesses that were more common south of the Himalayas. He wondered if the habit of tea-drinking had something to do with it. Typically, he speculated on the possibility of beginning a great indigenous tea industry native to the Himalayan region.

He had more patients in Leh than he could cope with, including those who needed the usual advice on ophthalmic, surgical and rheumatic problems. By the end of his first winter there, Moorcroft wrote that of the 'many' patients considered 'incurable' by local doctors, he had lost only two. Soon, his reputation had spread across the Karakoram, and even to Yarkand and beyond.

Moorcroft hoped to end the smallpox scourge beyond the Himalayas. He had been trying to introduce vaccination there since his first visit to Tibet in 1812. On that occasion, his first meeting with the suspicious 'Khalun', the administrative head at Ladakh, had not been successful. By the end of that first winter in Leh, however, he had earned a lot of goodwill, and so managed to train a sufficient number of vaccinators.

His patients came bearing gifts that soon formed a small fortress around him. Piles of wheat cakes, lumps of yak butter, bags of roasted barley wheat, and heaps of onions. There were wooden bowls filled with milk, yogurt, large teapots of buttered tea and flagons of *chhang* (a kind of barley beer), and once, even a sheep tied to a stone.

Chimneys of Ladakh

Moorcroft was appalled at the acrid smoke from the yak-dung fires that filled every Ladakhi living room in winter. He often insisted the fire be put out. He would have to lie on the floor to clear his streaming eyes before he could treat some of his patients. All this for the want of a chimney!

Moravian missionaries from Central Europe, who came to Ladakh a few decades later won the gratitude of the people by introducing the stove and chimney. It made the long winters bearable and got rid of the smoke and the inconvenience of boring a hole in the ceiling.

The Journey Westward

After a long delay in Ladakh, as he waited for a resolution to his financial situation, Moorcroft decided to move ahead to Bukhara via the west and turned again towards Kashmir. The previous eighteen months alone had cost him roughly three times his salary in that period. But it was at Kunduz in north-eastern Afghanistan, then ruled by a power-hungry and suspicious king, that Moorcroft found himself tragically outmanoeuvred.

He travelled with his party through Gilgit and Baltistan in the northern Himalayas, Peshawar and Waziristan (in present-day Pakistan) and Bamiyan in Afghanistan, before heading northward towards Afghanistan's border with the kingdoms of Central Asia. In Waziristan, he didn't find the horses he desired, but once again his medical practice thrived. Despite the nearby presence of a Sufi saint said to have a gift of healing, Moorcroft noticed with amusement that the difficult medical cases were always passed on to him. Many of these were the result of savage sword wounds that came from the long persisting blood feuds between clans.

At Bamiyan, he wrote of the huge Buddha figures, where, as a later writer recounts, he scratched his name on the rock, having climbed up to get a better view. All this travel took another several months.

At Tashkurghan (present-day Kholm), he encountered Murad Beg, the ruler of this area between Kholm and Kunduz. Murad Beg was outwardly friendly, as he informed Moorcroft that he had arranged for the whole party to come to Kunduz where their goods would be safe from thieves. Murad Beg, however, intended to make enquiries into the truth about Moorcroft being a genuine merchant and horse dealer. It was a specious reason to delay him, but Moorcroft was by this time desperate. Many of his companions were sick. But they were now virtually prisoners, utterly dependent on what the chief decided.

Murad Beg finally agreed to let them pass towards Bukhara, but only after a payment of 50,000 rupees. The persuasive diplomacy of Mir Wazir Ahmed, a local noble, reduced this sum to 10,000 rupees that included a sum of 2,000 rupees to Atma Ram, Murad Beg's wazir.

A PORTRAIT SAID TO BE OF ATMA RAM, MURAD BEG'S WAZIR

Destination: Bukhara

After a long and laborious pilgrimage of more than five years, Moorcroft finally gazed at the domes and minarets of Bukhara with relief and pleasure. But it was here that Moorcroft would spend the next, and almost the last, five months of his life. In 1825, a frosty February and March gave way to a wet and chilly April and then, from early May, all rain stopped. Then came a furnace-like heat.

Emir Khan Haydar (Haydar Bin Shahmurad), the ruler of Bukhara, was away from the city at the time of Moorcroft's arrival but, two days after his return, Moorcroft was summoned to the fort and led along with George Trebeck through long courtrooms, corridors and galleries to the great hall of public audience. The emir was 'gloomy and suspicious', as Moorcroft described him, along with a 'ticklish temper'. The ruler's irrational, high-pitched laughter and his bizarre, inconsistent behaviour made Moorcroft wonder about his sanity. Yet his power was absolute and he was greatly feared by everyone around him. Like many tyrants, his rule thrived with an army of secret police, spies and informers.

Horses for Courses

Although the emir had given him permission to trade for horses, the horse brokers Moorcroft tried to negotiate with refused to sell their horses without specific authority. He had to go back to petition the king once more. He was tiring of the whims of despots he had to negotiate and plead with.

The emir did accord his British visitor some privileges, which had never before been granted to foreign merchants or 'infidels'. Moorcroft could ride his horse into the city through its gates without dismounting. He was granted a permit forbidding any interference in his efforts to purchase horses and allowing the remission of all duties on his merchandise.

Unfortunately, it soon became apparent to Moorcroft that long years of warfare, raiding and anarchy, similar to what he had already witnessed further south, had left the kingdom of Bukhara in dire straits. Uncertainty had affected the horse trade. The teeming bazaars that had once made Bukhara a commercial hub, a centre of trade through the Silk Road, were now mostly empty. Moorcroft still held out hope, however, of some high-quality horses. The court's wealthy men had some remarkably fine animals in their stables.

Luck was not on his side, though. Moorcroft was just embarking on the long process of inspection, negotiation and purchase, when the emir suddenly called together his chiefs and soldiers, and departed over 100 miles (160 kilometres) to the east. There had been a sudden rebellion by a semi-nomadic tribe on the road to Samarkand. Moorcroft was present at the grand parade as the army departed. This included many horses, including almost all the best animals he had earmarked for purchase. It must have been a bittersweet experience for him. He had come so far to get the horses he desired, only to see them led off into battle.

A Long Wait

Till early June, Moorcroft waited for the emir's return, and then his fear of being caught by yet another cruel and long-stretching winter convinced him that he had to leave. He had already been in Bukhara for five months. He could not get quite the number of horses he had wished for.

THE 'MOST WANTED' YARKANDI OR TURKOMAN HORSE

After crossing the Oxus (the Amu Darya) on his way back, around 4 or 5 August 1825, Moorcroft suddenly decided to take a different route and to head to Maymana in Afghanistan, where he hoped to find the horses of his dreams. He was truly obsessed with them and desperate to make good on his claims.

On the morning of 18 August 1825, Moorcroft's little party rode away from the rest of his caravan, whom he instructed to wait for him at Balkh. His companions saw him head out across the cold desert and that was the last they saw of him. Moorcroft never returned, not to his waiting friends at Balkh, nor to India. A later traveller, Abbe Hue, reported 12 years later that Moorcroft had been sighted in Lhasa where he lived for several years, but there was never anything more to this story.

2

MANY DISGUISES, MANY LANDS

MOHAN LAL KASHMIRI TRAVELS INTO THE UNKNOWN

A gift for blending in and a flair for languages helped Mohal Lal Zutshi get to places not frequented by Indians at the time, and record events, escapes and escapades!

Barely five years after William Moorcroft's unhappy journey to Bukhara, a young man of Kashmiri origin, Mohan Lal, travelled there. Mohan Lal Zutshi or Mohan Lal 'Kashmiri' accompanied the English explorer, scholar and spy, Alexander Burnes, as an interpreter and assistant. He journeyed through the same badlands as Moorcroft and lived to tell the tale.

Making a Good Impression

In his accounts, written after his travels, Mohan Lal talks of kings and commoners, the riches and luxuries enjoyed by some, while others lived in dire misery; the generosity of some rulers, contrasted by the bigotry of others; the kindness of strangers, and the downright suspicion shown by many. He travelled, changing guise often, taking on different names and identities, and assuming different habits. It made him, as he wrote in his book, a well-travelled man, and yet an 'outcaste' within his own community, because he travelled to strange lands and dined with people of other religions.

The strange turns in his life began when, as a young man and student at the Delhi College, he impressed Alexander Burnes with his recitation of an English poem on the division of Poland. It showed not just his fluency in English but a familiarity with world events. Burnes, who was keen to explore the north-western part of the subcontinent for political and intellectual reasons, and to help the East India Company map unknown lands, offered him the job as his secretary right away. Mohan Lal, with his knowledge of English and Persian, and his loyalty, soon made himself indispensable.

Early Days in Delhi

He was born in 1812 in Delhi, and was nineteen when he left with Burnes, heading for the kingdoms of Central Asia. This first journey in 1831 would take three years. He would return in 1834, travelling via Iran and Afghanistan. In 1838, he went with Burnes again to Kabul, where the latter had been appointed the British Resident in a time of turmoil. In the aftermath of the First Anglo-Afghan War in 1841, which ended badly for the British, Mohan Lal was witness to Burnes's tragic murder and death.

In his introduction to Mohan Lal Kashmiri's book, C.F. Trevelyan, who had once been his English teacher at the

MOHAN LAL: THE 'CATCH-ME-IF-YOU CAN' MAN

Delhi College, described him as 'a fine and picturesque specimen of the man of the East'. Trevelyan praised his intelligence and spirit.

Mohan Lal's grandfather was a mid-ranking Mughal noble and once held a considerable estate. But as Mughal power declined, so did the fortunes of Mohan Lal's family. His father, Rae Budh Singh, continued to reside in Delhi, despite these reverses. But Budh Singh proved adaptable to changing circumstances, and Mohan Lal would be as well. Budh Singh served as Persian secretary to the British officer and later Governor of Bombay Presidency, Mountstuart Elphinstone, and travelled with him to Peshawar. He understood the benefits of an English education in a time of change and encouraged his son, who had been taught Persian at home, to join an English class just established in the Persian college at Delhi. In 1828, Mohan Lal was among the first batch of six boys to study English.

Three years later, in December 1831, came Mohan Lal's momentous meeting with Alexander Burnes, who offered him a position on a salary of Rs 1,000 per annum. Mohan Lal had never been away from Delhi. He was warned by friends and well-wishers alike that the journey, mostly on horseback, could be

ALEXANDER BURNES, IN DISGUISE

dangerous. The roads and public highways could be infested with thieves and robbers, and the lands they would visit were known for their hostility towards the British. Yet Mohan Lal was young and enthusiastic, and totally up for an adventure.

Through the Punjab

Once they crossed the River Sutlej, they were in the territory of Maharaja Ranjit Singh of Punjab, who when informed of their arrival, sent a friendly letter to Burnes.

On 12 January 1832, they were at a place in Punjab's Tarn Taran district where they visited a stud of mares belonging to Ranjit Singh. Mohan Lal described them as 'smart and beautiful'. The story goes that a Muslim saint had once cured horses struck by a serious illness, and the Sikhs in gratitude had repaired and beautified the mosque where he prayed. Burnes called the Sikhs most tolerant in their religion.

They had their first meeting with Ranjit Singh in Lahore some days later. 'In such a fine tent he held his darbar as if it was the tent of an angel and not of man,' wrote Mohan Lal. The maharaja received them at the door, seated Burnes and Dr James Gerard, who too was part of the journey, in golden chairs and engaged in friendly conversation with them.

Lahore was a fortified town with a deep moat running round it. The streets were narrow and muddy, and one could not pass through 'without dirtying his trousers and shoes.' A few days later, they accompanied the king on a hunting excursion.

The Basant Festival

On 6 February, the famous festival of Basant was celebrated with a great show at the shrine of Haqiqat Rai, four miles from Lahore. The Sikh troops, clad in yellow, lined the road on both sides. Then the Maharaja, dressed in yellow robes and accompanied by his European officers, rode to the yellow silk tents, which had floors laid with carpets from Kashmir. Each tent had a camp bed, curtains of yellow silk and matching coverlets.

Leaving Lahore three days later, they crossed the River Ravi in a ferry boat and halted at Shahdara for the night. They had considerably reduced their baggage and helpers for fear of attracting the attention of local robbers. Burnes and Gerard were already in 'Punjabi dress' with heavy turbans, long shirts and loose trousers. They wore slippers without socks and were at ease sitting cross-legged on the ground.

Punjab was safe and peaceful, but things were different on its outskirts. The land on the western bank of the Jhelum was barren and poverty-stricken, and people found it difficult to provide for their families.

The next month, they arrived at Rawalpindi and put up in the house of Shah Shuja, the former king of Kabul, who had been deposed by Dost Mohammad. Now

MAHARAJA RANJIT SINGH AND SOLDIERS, ALL DRESSED IN YELLOW

they put on Afghan dresses, pretending to be from the Durrani tribe. They also changed their names; Burnes called himself Sikandar Khan and Mohan Lal adopted the name Hasan Jan.

Deep in the Badlands

They crossed the River Indus on elephants and reached Peshawar where they received a cordial reception from its governor, Sultan Muhammad Khan. Peshawar was not a fortified town. Its streets were paved, and wider and cleaner than those of Lahore. A number of brooks crossed by bridges ran through the town.

SULTAN MOHAMMAD KHAN

Mohan Lal described the governor as being a careless and vain ruler who liked to adorn himself in splendid and precious robes. Burnes, however, found him educated and well-bred, and his 'open and affable manner' made a lasting impression on Burnes.

Burnes carried his money carefully, for fear of it being stolen. A loss would make things difficult for the journey ahead as well. For instance, he fastened to his left arm a letter of credit – if he was ever in need of a loan – for five thousand rupees. It was hidden away like an amulet. As he had to keep his identity secret, he tied his passport to his right arm, and around his waist was securely tied a bag of gold coins. He also distributed a part of his money for safekeeping to each of the helpers, who were trustworthy and would never betray him.

After a month-long stay, the party left Peshawar. They were joined on the way by numerous travellers, so they came to form a fairly large caravan. On 26 April, they reached Jalalabad in Afghanistan where they saw a magnificent Hindu temple, named Gorakh Nath, which was full of pilgrims, and pigeons.

Mohan Lal explored the town thoroughly. The inhabitants spoke Persian, but Pashto was the more common language. The Hindus numbered nearly 2,000 and, according to him, were 'allowed to keep all the privileges of their religion'. They were treated tolerantly

THE BAMIYAN STATUES OF BUDDHA AS MOHAN LAL MIGHT HAVE SEEN THEM

and had their shops in all streets and bazaars, not in any separate quarters.

Bamiyan was famous for its colossal idols. Three images, as Moorcroft too had noted, were cut out of solid rock and stood on the hard face of the mountain. The idols were more than 100 feet in height. On one side of the idols, Mohan Lal recorded, there were a considerable number of caves.

The Tyrants of Central Asia

Leaving Bamiyan towards the end of May, the party made its way through the passes of the Hindukush mountain range. Many in the party fearing this passage – into territory known to be hostile and dangerous, because of the fierce tribesmen who lived beyond – now turned back, but Mohan Lal, loyal as ever to Burnes, besides being conscientious and curious, carried on.

Soon after, they entered Turkistan. Mohan Lal still kept up his disguise, as did the others, but there were those who saw through his ruse. A merchant, Chiman Das, invited Mohan Lal to dinner. When he asked Mohan Lal about the nature of his journey, the latter lied that he was in search of a long-lost brother. Chiman Das laughed to his face and told him that he knew Mohan Lal was 'the *munshi* [secretary/clerk] attached to the *firangis*', but that he would not disclose this secret to anyone.

Murad Beg, the country's ruler and the persecutor of Moorcroft, was a short man of thin stature. He had 'very small and gloomy eyes', and 'except for a few hairs on his chin', he had no beard. He had many slave girls and boys. His diwan or prime minister, Atma Ram, was known to be capable and shrewd.

On their way to Kholm, where only some years ago, Moorcroft had been held hostage for several months, they disguised themselves as poor, indigent travellers. They 'never changed clothes till they disappeared under filth and vermin', they slept in dark rooms, full of dung, and ate stale bread. The sleeves of their shirts served as towels, and fingernails as combs for the hair. At Kholm, Mohan Lal was present at the market day when slaves were sold in an open and large shop. It made for a miserable experience. He noted how the young people there cried uncontrollably as they were 'exhibited' for sale, and even older men stood about in a sad and dejected mood.

On 2 June, they received news that Murad Beg would receive them in his camp near Kunduz, seventy miles away. This alarmed them for the ruler was not well inclined towards English travellers. Mohan Lal, in tears, entreated Chiman Das to step in, and the merchant, already sympathetic towards Mohan Lal, agreed. He spoke to the Mir himself, who gave them permission to leave.

They left in the company of a body of horsemen provided by Chiman Das. After Mazar-e-Sharif, they arrived at Balkh on the 9 June.

The Desert Ride

They crossed the River Oxus (Amu Darya) ten days later on boats pulled by horses. Then they journeyed on camels through an arid, waterless desert. It was extremely hot, and they travelled cooped up in camel baskets about four feet long and three feet wide, and covered in blankets that gave little protection against the sun and flying sand. Mohan Lal wrote of how his parched lips and dry throat rendered him speechless.

On 21 June, the day of the solstice, the longest day of summer, they came across some Turkomans in their tents, and large herds of cattle. Their food generally consisted of bread, curd, and meat, and to the weary travellers, this seemed like manna from heaven.

Finally, they arrived at Bukhara on 27 June. Mohan Lal found the rulers strict about matters of religion, and anyone flouting customs was punished and humiliated in public. The people were also chastised in public for smoking, snorting tobacco and drinking.

Mohan Lal's observations about the customs, manners and practices of the people of Bukhara are very interesting. He found them to be good riders, able to withstand hunger, cold and fatigue for long periods as they travelled out in the desert. They wore two or three cloaks and white turbans. People of certain communities were not allowed to ride on horseback or to wear a shawl or a piece of cloth round their waist but were obliged to use just a plain rope or string instead, and a black cap on the head.

The shops usually opened after nine o'clock in the morning, as their owners emerged only after they had had tea. The large, roofed bazaar had a striking appearance. The shops, which followed each other in a straight line presented a splendid sight, with all kinds of goods, ranging from ornaments to chinaware, on display.

A Persian Prince

Burnes's intention was to study in secret the political situation in the regions he travelled to. Some six months later, the party reached Herat in Afghanistan, and received a warm welcome from the wazir, Din Muhammad Khan Sardar. Mohan Lal stayed here till 3 February 1833, when he was deputed by Burnes to head west to Mashhad in Iran for financial help (with the use of a letter of credit), and some urgently needed medicines as James Gerard had fallen sick.

During their time in Herat, the ruler, Shah Kamran, granted several interviews to Gerard and Mohan Lal, and to the latter, he always appeared intoxicated with opium. He also taxed his subjects unmercifully.

Several months later, in September of 1833, they reached the holy city of Mashhad in north-eastern Iran where they stayed as guests of an Armenian lady. The ever-curious Mohan Lal attempted to examine a public bath that was exclusively reserved for Muslims. He was almost detected as there were many in the travelling caravan who already knew his real identity. His Persian costume and his assumed diction, however, saved him. When he visited the sacred tombs, he imitated every gesture of his fellow pilgrims and managed to get away unscathed.

Soon after, on the holy occasion of Eid, Mohan Lal and James Gerard were invited to the palace by the prince, Abbas Mirza. The prince, fascinated by their stories, asked him about Ranjit Singh. Could Ranjit Singh's court vie in magnificence with what Mohan Lal now saw before him, the prince asked, and could the Sikh army compare in discipline and courage with the Persian troops?

ABBAS MIRZA

Mohan Lal answered as tactfully as possible. Maharaja Ranjit Singh's darbar tent was made of Kashmir shawls and even the floor was lined with such expensive material. As for his army, if Sardar Hari Singh (the king's commander-in-chief) were to cross the River Indus, the prince would soon see for himself the strength of the Punjab army and retreat to Tabriz, which was farther away and more secure than Mashhad. The prince was taken aback, and yet amused and impressed by such a candid reply.

Later, Mohan Lal wrote of being detained at both Herat and Mashhad, for there was some suspicion that they were Russian spies, and then Gerard fell very sick. Burnes at this time remained in Bukhara.

Days after Mohan Lal left with Gerard, they were attacked by robbers, who succeeded in seizing two camels loaded with goods including all of Mohan Lal's papers, and some English goods, such as swords, brought as presents for the Kandahar chiefs. It was meant to be a bribe in exchange for safe passage to India.

Kandahar was noted for the quality of its fruits. For a 'pice', several seers of grapes could be purchased; and figs, plums, apricots, peaches, pears, melons, pomegranates and almonds were nearly as cheap.

They reached Kabul on 5 November and were invited to dinner by Dost Muhammad Khan, the ruler of Kabul. Mohan Lal visited Babur's tomb and was fascinated by the sight of it. The panoramic view of the square in which the tomb was situated, shaded by fruit trees of different kinds and washed by numerous canals, charmed him so much that he stood motionless, wondering if he was dreaming or travelling in a wonderland.

The King of Afghanistan

DOST MOHAMMAD, RULER OF KABUL

He described Dost Mohammad as a tall man of haughty appearance. His proud tone of speech and plain dress indicated his high rank and sovereign power. He trusted no one and was surrounded by enemies, both within the court and without. Dost Mohammad was not someone who would extend a permanent friendship or political alliance to anyone, and was known to have killed many chiefs of the country and deprived many of their estates. He wanted to make himself the sole monarch of Afghanistan and destroy his rivals. Yet, he needed allies and supporters to meet his perpetual need for money.

The British were wary of him, and their plan to dislodge him with a more pliable ruler, Shah Shuja, set off the First Anglo-Afghan War in 1838.

At Jalalabad, Mohan Lal went excavating with Gerard. They had heard much about the old ruins that were scattered in abundance here. They did find a considerable number of old Grecian coins. After five days of toiling, they managed to dig up some ancient artefacts. Among these was an image cut out of black stone; it had matted locks of hair flowing over its shoulders, and held on either shoulder two mace bearers.

The Terrible Riots in Kabul

After he reached Delhi, Burnes gave him a glowing recommendation, describing Mohan Lal as a 'young man of great promise' who could easily stand out among his countrymen.

He accompanied Burnes again to Kabul in 1841. In 1838, Burnes had been knighted by Queen Victoria for his services. This visit was ill-fated, for the Afghans resented the British who had overthrown Dost Mohammad and installed Shah Shuja. Mohan Lal informed Burnes about the rumours in the marketplace. There were plans that Burnes's residence would be stormed by a mob, yet Burnes stayed put, refusing to leave even when hostile crowds appeared at his door. He was killed, but Mohan Lal managed a narrow escape.

In 1844, Mohan Lal left for a visit to England. He sailed in an East India Company steam frigate towards the port of Suez, and then took the Mediterranean route to reach Southampton in England. Friends, especially the East India Company's junior officials who knew him, welcomed him warmly.

Meeting a Queen in London

Mohan Lal was quite bewildered in London. He was puzzled to see the crowds of people, travelling in carriages, carts and cabs, all along the wide, long and clean streets. These were all illuminated, and the shops had a rich and amazing variety of things.

The houses were regularly built, but small, and hot, as the windows were always shut. He never kept the windows of his bedroom shut, and the curtains too were never drawn. England was, he wrote, not as cold as the people pretended. He always wore a thin shirt and white trousers. The ballrooms were always terribly heated, and he once fainted when in one. Despite this, he claimed to like the climate very much and that his health had improved on his visit.

The winter fog and the smoke that prevailed over London were the only things he complained about. In the country, on the other hand, the air was pure and delightful.

Sir Alexander Burnes's father invited Mohan Lal, 'the faithful friend of his lamented son', to visit him in Montrose, Scotland. It was a sorrowful meeting, full of reminiscences about the man they both missed. Mohan Lal stopped for a short time in Edinburgh as well. He had his portrait painted by Sir William Allan, the well-known artist. From Glasgow, he travelled to Ireland, and found it beautiful and green. He was distressed, though, at some of the poverty he witnessed.

The land and the people towards the county of Sligo, in north Ireland, were very poor, he wrote. It was heart-rending to see men and women, with large families, walking without shoes and sufficient clothing despite the piercing cold. The poor inhabitants appeared to be living entirely on potatoes, and he realized Ireland was a country in some distress.

When he returned to London, Prince Albert, the Prince Consort, extended an invitation to him. Mohan Lal also met Queen Victoria and was invited to a court ball. The importance accorded to him filled him with ecstasy. As he wrote, the hall became brighter and more beautiful when Her Majesty, Queen Victoria, and her royal consort, Prince Albert, arrived to take part in the dance. The queen appeared very graceful as she danced.

Mohan Lal's book received a lot of attention from his British superiors. His own countrymen and relatives in Delhi, perhaps envious of his fortune and travels, accused him of defiling his caste, and breaking caste norms by travelling and living with people from other communities. For the next thirty years, he lived a relatively quiet life in Delhi. His wife, Hydari Begum, was well-read and was known to have kept a diary of events during the Great Revolt of 1857 in Delhi.

3

IN THE LAND OF GOLDEN PAGODAS

COLESWORTHY GRANT IN THE EAST

An artist, writer and a friend of ill-treated animals – what was his purpose in travelling all the way to Burma?

To the British in nineteenth century India, Burma – now called Myanmar – to the east appeared to be a fabled land, one where rubies and precious jewels could be found in plenty, where white elephants roamed the jungles, and towering pagodas rose above forests and towns. But there were more practical concerns for British interest in Burma.

Burma promised to be an endless source of timber for the many construction activities the British intended in India, more so once railway lines began to be built from the 1850s onward. Burma was also a land where rice was widely grown.

The First Anglo-Burmese War of 1824 secured many concessions for the British, such as total control of the areas now making up Assam, Manipur and parts of Nagaland. As part of the Treaty of Yandabo, the

Tanintharyi coast (Tenasserim), along with Arakan, was ceded to Britain.

Yet, the British wanted more privileges for trade and remained suspicious of the Burmese king. The French influence at the court of Siam (Thailand), south of Burma, was growing, and the British were anxious to make their position in Burma more assured and definite.

A Travelling Artist

In 1846, twenty years or so after the first war, when things were still in a flux, a young English artist, Colesworthy Grant, then in Calcutta (now Kolkata), travelled on a small ship headed for Burma. Grant had no fixed plans. He had, in his belongings, things he loved, especially his sketchbook and drawing pencils. For Grant was an artist, who had taught himself to sketch and paint. Since 1838, he had been contributing sketches to various magazines like the *Indian Review* and the *Calcutta Monthly Journal*. He also illustrated medical books such as *Mouat's Annals of Anatomy*. Several of the city's important figures wanted their portraits painted by him.

COLESWORTHY GRANT

He was only nineteen when he first sailed out from England to India. Grant came to the subcontinent to join his brother, George, a clockmaker as well as an entertaining mimic. Their father had had a business making mathematical instruments, but later went on stage to perform comedy. In their different ways, with mimicry or music, the family knew how to entertain people.

The Calcutta Mechanics Institute (later, the Calcutta School of Art) was established in 1839, and both George and Colesworthy were its honorary secretaries. It had a library, and offered instruction in mathematics, measurements and the basic sciences. Grant took classes free of charge, every Wednesday evening and on Saturdays, lecturing students on 'perspective', so essential for artists. He taught drawing at the engineering college at Howrah, and for some time also taught the subject at the civil engineering department in Presidency College.

Grant had other talents too. He was the Calcutta correspondent for the *Durham Advertiser* of which another of his brothers, J.G. Grant, was editor. The short pieces he wrote to his sisters later became a book called *Rural Life in Bengal*. In 1861, he was involved in something more enduring, when he helped set up the Calcutta Society for the Prevention of Cruelty to Animals. Grant was particularly disturbed by injuries that horses and bullocks suffered when they pulled overloaded wagons.

A Friendly Visit

In 1846, when he was thirty-four, Grant accepted an invitation from a friend to visit Burma. Later, he wrote about his visit in 1853, and the book contained his many sketches of the journey. The monsoons had just broken as they set off. The little schooner, called *Flora Macdonald*, which they would travel in, was noted in Calcutta for being the smartest and smallest craft to ever sail out of the port. But his journey to Moulmein was anything but comfortable.

It was marked by incidents, troubles, and dangers more than, as Grant wrote, what a traveller might face in a dozen voyages to England and back again in a large ship. The schooner, despite its size, had a spacious cabin, yet it was stuffed with excess cargo that had improperly been sent on board by people. It was a clear instance of illegal trade the Burmese authorities were wary of. Crammed 'in sweet confusion', as Colesworthy wrote, were a collection of large cases, chests, bags, stores, beds, bundles and sails. A gale set in right after they left, and Grant joined others in 'kedging' – hauling a ship using oars – to pull it out of tight harbours. The sandbanks were close and very treacherous.

Meetings at Moulmein

As they neared Moulmein in early August 1846, the port town presented an inviting appearance. Moulmein served as the first capital of British Burma during 1826–52. The European residences were entirely hidden behind a series of low Burmese buildings – the bazaar, wharfs and merchants' warehouses. Beautiful blue hills covered with luxuriant greenery seen from afar served as a charming background, despite the untidily arranged shacks and warehouses nearer the shore. Used to the flat plains of Bengal for fourteen years, Grant was moved by this sight.

His host, Captain Miller, lived in a traditional Burmese house built of the finest teak wood, enough to have built a big gunship! The house was attached to the timber premises known as Boothby's Yard. Timber of every description, great and small, was scattered in every direction. These were carried toward the water by a continuous procession of elephants.

The rain was frequent and heavy, and Colesworthy spent his time sketching indoors. He did put in a visit to the large and picturesque pagoda on the summit

A 'Penang-Lawyer'

The next day, they were at Amherst, now called Kyankkhami. His companions, wishing to hunt ashore, armed themselves with guns, but Grant being a poor shot and not very inclined to the sport, contented himself with a thin, quite durable walking stick, called the 'Penang-lawyer' as it was made of palm grown in Malaysia and Singapore (Penang being a place further south from Burma). This stick would remain with him through his later adventures in Burma. He also had his pencil and a sheet of paper, more in keeping with his interests.

of Pagoda Hill. Rudyard Kipling would refer to it later as the 'old Moulmein Pagoda' and it's today known as the Kyaik Than Lan, or Kyaikthanlan Pagoda. Its location high on a hill provides a grand view of the city. It is ranged by thirty-four smaller pagodas, and prized for containing among its treasures, a hair relic of the Buddha and a tooth relic, which were gifted by Sri Lanka in the ancient period.

He visited the grave of a young woman missionary, Ann Judson, who had been one of the first foreigners who came to Burma. She was revered for standing by her husband despite the persecution he suffered at the hands of the Burmese authorities.

ANN JUDSON

Colesworthy sketched a bit while he was there: Noble trees – clusters of giant bamboos – and luxuriant vegetation of every kind, the graceful pagodas, the paths bordered by rich flowering jungle and deep woody banks sloping down to the blue sea, which always looked serene and beautiful.

On one occasion, he came upon a herd of buffaloes, an animal he had been warned about. These buffaloes, however, turned out to be docile. But this docility, he felt, was deceptive, quite like that of a sleeping alligator or a gorged boa constrictor.

The Sights of Rangoon

He wasn't very impressed with much of Rangoon but was full of praise for the beauty of its principal feature: the Great or Golden Pagoda.

Rangoon (Yangon) was about twenty-eight miles inland from the sea. The pagoda was visible as they came up the river that bears its name, and the view was marvellous on a fine day. Its graceful form rose prominently over dense and elevated forest land. The golden brightness was enhanced on a closer view. Nearer the town, smaller pagodas appeared, surrounded by clusters of huts, including several superior and picturesque-looking buildings with upper stories. These latter were the residences of the *poongees* or Burmese priests. Only high priests and royal personages had the honour of having extensive dwelling places.

The town was like a vast assemblage of wooden huts. It was surrounded by a wooden stockade, 16 to 18 feet in height, with no view of the fine river that ran past. The stockade added to the town's confined and unhealthy appearance.

The few brick houses that were there belonged to Europeans, who needed special permits to construct them. It was, Grant wrote, the policy of the Court of Ava (the Burmese capital) to prevent, as much as possible, both foreigners and natives from having houses built with permanent materials. The strange belief was that these could become places of resistance, in which their rebellious subjects could take shelter and oppose laws.

Grant described the packs of hungry and noisy dogs that were a source of dread in the day, and of disturbance at night. The huts and houses visible from the river were made of wood, the larger kind with roofs of the same material, while the smaller ones had thatched roofs. The floors were built high on wooden posts, to protect against rising floodwaters. At high tide, houses near the riverbank looked as if they were afloat.

A Rich Man's House

Grant's first visit in Rangoon was to the house of the young Armenian owner of the *Flora McDonald*, G.S. Manook. This house was the most conspicuous building on the riverbank. They entered through a little portico that led to an immense apartment from end to end. There was wood everywhere – nothing but teak wood on the floor, walls and roof – and not a whiff of paint on any portion of it. The windows had Venetian shades, like the Calcutta houses of the time, but not an atom of glass. No glass was permitted in any other dwelling in Burma besides the king's palace.

The nature of the dwelling, and the damp atmosphere for most of the year, affected most articles of furniture or ornament, so the house was equipped with only those household conveniences that were essential. There was a table, with glasses and refreshments on it, a plain couch, a few chairs, and half a dozen coloured French prints on the walls. This apartment served as office, a gathering place, or even a gossip room to all visitors, especially the English commanders of ships in the river, and other Burmese merchants who had business to transact with Mr Manook.

Shortly after their arrival, a team of Burmese officials came to search the ship. They were entertained with rum and biscuits. There was, Grant wrote, one drawback to their comfort for they were quite in terror of the captain's dog, Jack. They sat, feet up on their chairs, and watched him carefully.

The main wharf, known as the king's wharf, was a massive pier with huge posts, to which a crane was attached at the outer end. On either side of the pier was a shed-like building with an ornamented roof. Along the riverside, there were a number of tall wooden posts, which were the remains of old wharfs the Burmese willfully set aflame after the English left the country in 1826.

A little further inland was the plain wooden spire of the Armenian Church, and then a Roman Catholic Church. In three different parts of the town there were mosques, indicating a large measure of tolerance.

Burmese Huts

The Burmese huts made of brick, wood and thatch resembled the comfortless looking houses in Calcutta's Burra Bazaar. The residence of the ship's captain, Hugh Brown, was something totally unexpected. His house had a thatched roof, but it was otherwise made almost entirely of brick, stone and iron. It was indeed one of the most solid and substantial edifices Grant had seen yet in Burma. Its floors and steps were laid with stone, and it had strong iron doors with massive fastenings. The windows, with their iron bars, were like small embrasures usually seen in a fort. The house was nicknamed the 'Prison' simply because of its appearance, but the captain did fear two things: fire and thieves.

The Burmese, though partial to roses, with which the women decorated their beautiful black hair, were not much given to garden cultivation. Gourds and fruit trees were cared for, but there was nothing in the shape of flower beds or decorative shrubs. Everything appeared to be jungle. Good taste did appear, Grant noted, in other aspects, in the manner the pagodas, priests' houses and some other dwellings were constructed. Grant was impressed by the fact that a 'head-servant's' house was done up as carefully as some of the native bungalows in Bengal.

The Burmese hut had a neat and square thatched roof fastened with stalks of bamboo, and its grated doors and neatly fashioned garden rails gave it a European look. Silk and cotton plaid fabrics, wooden and leather shoes, ear ornaments, betel-nut cutters, and 'Burma boxes', a prized item for many in India, were staple commodities in most houses.

A BURMESE LADY PAINTED BY GRANT

The Great Pagoda

The Great Pagoda was gilded (coated with gold) from base to summit. It was built upon a natural hill and was enveloped in a dark dense mass of luxuriant foliage, mainly consisting of peepul, tamarind, palm and coconut trees. The gilding was renewed every eight years at enormous expense. The vale around the pagoda was covered with luxuriant jungle, with stunted palm trees, and a perfect forest of small pagodas, many of these being higher than the smaller palm trees.

On the left, hidden by trees, was a gilded portico – the southern entrance to the pagoda. Right at the approach, the road sloped down. through a village, and several ruined pagodas literally buried in vegetation. In the pagoda's neighbourhood appeared a tank crammed with small fish, and a *ziyat* (a two-floored open pillared structure, as Grant describes) filled with marble figures of the Buddha, of every conceivable size and variety. In the centre was a gigantic Buddha statue around 12 or 15 feet in height, and around this were stationed in various attitudes of supplication – the hands joined and turned upwards, and with faces lifted toward the principal figure – rows of smaller images, varying in size from six feet to about as many inches. These were packed as closely as books on a shelf. Several images appeared mutilated.

Once Grant proceeded around the base of the hill (sinking nearly up to the knees in swamp and wet grass) to the main entrance, he walked up a long flight of steps overlain by a gilded portico for the most part. When he came to the base of the pagoda itself, he was not allowed to advance, for the priests understood that he practised a different religion.

Just ahead lay a handsome archway with elaborately carved woodwork. Within were rows of large burning candles attended to by the priests. It happened to be a festival day, and almost the town's entire population had gathered, gaily dressed in their best, carrying baskets of food, flowers and fruit offerings to the Buddha, many carefully wending their way along the several paths to the pagoda.

These roads were paved with brick. But several of Rangoon's streets were in urgent need of repair.

Grant did not get permission to portray the king nor could he sketch the priests. He did sketch some important state officials, but most of his pictorial efforts

AMARAPURA PALACE PAINTED BY GRANT

were confined to landscapes, and he found loads of material to arrest his attention and curtail his walks. Indeed, the countryside around Rangoon, with its rich greenery, pretty lakes and hills, and innumerable pagodas, some perfect in their simple and yet graceful architecture, and others in every possible stage of decay – more than made up for the imperfections, Grant felt, that lay elsewhere in the town.

Every time he sat down to sketch, he was often surrounded by the Burmese – not just by men but women and girls too, who looked over his shoulder, and tried to engage in conversation with him. They seemed very amused by Grant's efforts and appeared to perfectly understand him.

Burmese Boats

After the pagodas, the Burmese displayed great skill in boat manufacture. The length of the boats varied from 40 to 50 feet, and their breadth from about five to 10 feet. They were mostly covered with bamboo and mat-work, and used for travelling and to carry cargo. The most conspicuous object was the steersman's (chief boatman) seat, which was an elaborately carved chair, in which the helmsman sat with all the dignity of a ruler.

The timber used to make the boats was not teak, but a heavy and durable wood, known locally as the *thengan*. Many, however, were also made from the *pyeema*, which in India was called the *jarul* tree. The *jarul* tree was lofty and bore beautiful lilac flowers.

He had no opportunity of seeing the boats on which the Burmese prided themselves – their race boats. These boats were amazingly swift and performed the journey to Ava in six to eight days. The boats were manned by teams of athletic men, who displayed great spirit and bonhomie among themselves.

BEIN BRIDGE: A SLICE OF BURMESE LIFE

An Artist, but a Spy?

On one occasion, Grant found himself within a short distance of the Sule Pagoda, in the heart of downtown Yangon (of today), and he resolved to sketch it. He took up position on the grassy hollow between the road and a bund, or earthen wall, and his walking stick (the 'Penang lawyer') stuck in the mud beside him. He had completed about two-thirds of his sketch, when he turned around at the sudden sound of an angry Burmese voice. He found two men at his side. The elder appeared to be interrogating him about his intentions.

Barely had Grant extended his sketch towards him than he was disarmed of his stick by the interrogator. Grant assumed it was curiosity, the kind he was familiar with, and resumed his sketching, but the angry tone and gestures of the older man continued and soon the truth dawned on Grant. He realized he was suspected of being a spy!

The older man, flanked by an athletic young fellow, closed around Grant. He was marched through the town like a thief, with a small mob gathering at their heels. At the first place he was taken, the two sides did not speak the same language and so his interrogators could not understand his explanations. He was led a mile further to the court of a magistrate, who, on their arrival, was asleep and could not be disturbed.

Tearing a leaf out of his sketchbook, Grant addressed a brief note to his host, Captain Brown. But no one agreed to take his note and an insolent silence prevailed. Feeling like a mean pickpocket, exposed to the gaze of every passer-by, Grant waited some more time for an interpreter, who had been sent for, someone who spoke Hindustani. Strangely, there was no one who seemed to know English, and Grant, of course, did not know the local language.

By this time, the magistrate had made his appearance. He had an air of considerable importance, and reclined on a couch of pillows as he questioned Grant. The grave charges brought against him included, as Grant made out, ominous words like 'stranger' – 'foreign country' – 'war between the nations'– 'examining' – 'making writings of forts', among others. Grant tried to explain the harmlessness of his actions. The sketches of boats, men's heads, pots and pans, and even the fish he drew had nothing to do with war.

The magistrate recommended the case be referred a higher tribunal. A report was accordingly forwarded to the Governor of Rangoon, and in the meantime cheroots and fruit were offered in an odd mixture of oppression and hospitality! Grant rejected the offerings, assuring them he would not eat their bread while a prisoner. He was now asked if he could draw animals – and they asked him to make a likeness of a diabolical looking image or toy – half-human, half-demon, about three feet in height, and strung on most posts and columns.

A highly amused mob now surrounded him, with several women among them! It made him hopeful that he would not be hanged. The messenger returned at long last with the governor's order. A conversation was carried on between the magistrate and his advisers – mostly old men – and at last, Grant was informed that his explanation had been so 'good', and his words so 'sweet', that he was at liberty to go. As he left, marvelling at his escape, he heard someone running behind him. It was the interpreter hoping to get a fair remuneration for his services.

He returned to sketch the pagoda the next day itself, against the advice of his friends.

Once Again, Burma

On the day of Grant's departure from Burma with his friends, the authorities became suspicious and insisted on a check of their ship. Export of silver in any shape from Burma was strictly forbidden; most mercantile transactions were merely an exchange of commodities. There were even rumours that a war boat had been sent down to seize the *Flora McDonald*. But all dangers were tactfully averted and they did set off. Once he was back in Calcutta, Grant wrote of his pleasant voyage, and he wrote about liking the people he had met.

In 1855, he made a visit again, a more formal one when he accompanied Colonel Phayre, Lord Dalhousie's (then the British Governor General) representative on his

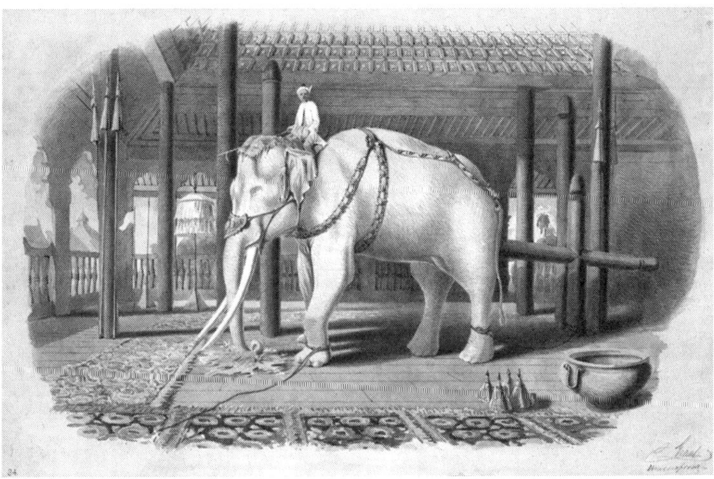

THE LORD WHITE ELEPHANT PAINTED BY GRANT: WHITE ELEPHANTS WERE CONSIDERED SYMBOLS OF GOOD FORTUNE AND POWER IN BURMA

official mission. This was soon after the second Anglo-Burma War during 1852–53, when the British accused, without much evidence, the Burmese of interfering in British trade activities in Burma. The British conquered Pegu and ransacked several pagodas including the Shwedagon Pagoda and the Gilded Stupa at Yangon.

Grant accompanied Phayre as an artist and Charles Linnaeus was the official photographer. The king was so impressed with Grant's drawings that he presented Grant with a gold cup and a ruby ring.

Grant returned to Calcutta and resumed his old life. It seems that an accident while exercising caused him an injury, and he was unable to walk erect for life. He continued sketching and drawing, and remained a popular figure.

4

FLOWER SPOTTER IN THE HIGH HILLS

JOSEPH DALTON HOOKER'S RHODODENDRONS

What can be more exciting for a botanist than finding an undiscovered flower species? Nothing, really – except for finding a few more!

As he trekked through Sikkim, Joseph Dalton Hooker noticed several species of a flowering shrub growing thick and dense, and in vivid shades of colour: purple, red, white and blue. Travelling further north all through that summer and early winter of 1849–50, he saw more of these flowers – hardy, resilient and wildly dense – even as it got colder around him.

As a scientist, Hooker knew these plants were part of the rhododendron family, but the many species he saw in Sikkim excited him. The rhododendron flowers seemed to be everywhere, growing at his feet, climbing along tree trunks, and some grew high like small trees! Hooker, who always had an eye for noting and recording new species, and a memory that helped him remember the exact spot where he had seen something, knew these flowers were unique and indigenous to the area.

JOSEPH DALTON HOOKER

He named them after people he knew. A very beautiful species, the *Rhododendron dalhousieae*, evoked the wife of the governor-general, Lord Dalhousie, with whom he had sailed out to India in 1848.

A particularly resilient species, the *Rhododendron barbatum*, found either as a shrub or as a tall tree (reaching as high as 18 metres), had a smooth mahogany-like red bark, spectacular red flowers and a leafstalk with bearded hair, and Hooker named the species accordingly: '*barbatum*' meaning a beard. When Hooker sent back seeds of these flowers to his father, then head of the Royal Gardens at Kew in England, they thrived, and were soon popular across estates in England and Ireland. Even the celebrated nurse Florence Nightingale planted them in her garden. Hooker named other species he found too, like a magnolia tree named *Magnolia campbellii* after his friend in Darjeeling, Archibald Campbell.

The notes he made, complete with details of plants he had seen and sketched, formed the basis for his book, *The Rhododendrons of Sikkim-Himalaya*, a beautifully illustrated work of flower-related literature of the nineteenth century.

A Geologist and His Ambitions

Joseph Dalton Hooker did not come to Sikkim on a whim or by accident. He had always had a special interest in geology and botany, and an intuitive understanding of how creatures gradually adapted to changing geological conditions or to the environment. Sikkim was rich in geographical diversity, much of it then still unexplored. Moreover, it occupied a strategic place between British India and Tibet. The ruler of Sikkim was seen as an ally by both the Tibetans and the British, and the latter were always anxious to extend their control over this region.

Hooker was asked to explore the eastern Himalayas. It was a strategic mission undoubtedly, but it was also scientific in intent. He was asked to look for fossil plants in these mountain regions. Cartography being another of Joseph Hooker's many skills, he was to (secretly) map the Kangchenjunga and the peaks around it as well as the many mountain valleys and passes that led to Tibet.

The Darwin Connection

When young, Hooker had an early fascination for science and all living creatures. In 1831, when he was only fourteen, he followed avidly, via newspaper accounts, the voyage of the HMS *Beagle* into the strange uncharted waters of the South Atlantic Ocean. The scientist on board, Charles Darwin, would later write a book about his travels and observations. Darwin's majestic magnum opus, *On the Origin of Species*, which dealt with evolution and interrelatedness of certain species, appeared in 1854 soon after Hooker himself had returned to England from India. This work radically changed the world of science. Later, Hooker would collaborate with Darwin on many projects.

Hooker's father William was also a biologist and the first official director of the Royal Botanical Gardens in Kew. Hooker himself would be the second. As a professor of botany at Glasgow University in Scotland, William Hooker was also known for his massive 'herbarium', which contained about a million dried plant specimens. Joseph's grandfather too had been a naturalist, and his maternal grandfather, Dawson Turner, was a banker who also collected insects.

PAGES FROM HOOKER'S *FLORA ANTARCTICA*

To Antarctica

On one of his first expeditions, Joseph Hooker was part of the team led by Captain James Clark Ross to Antarctica. He spent some time in the Falklands Islands in the Atlantic Ocean, east of Argentina, and was astounded by the library the British governor, Richard Clement Moody, had curated there. In 1846, drawn to other adventures, especially in the Himalayas, about which he had heard much, he left for India. By this time, he had started an informal correspondence with Charles Darwin.

A SCENE OF ANTARCTICA

He sailed by ship to Egypt, travelled overland from Alexandria to Suez in the days before the Suez Canal was built and then sailed to India. Hooker wrote about his travels through India once he reached Calcutta. He moved through eastern India towards Darjeeling, his base for his Himalayan journey, riding on elephants, carts and *palki*s. His *Himalayan Journals* were published after his return to England in 1854.

The King of Burdwan's Garden

The beginning of Hooker's journey in India saw him sail up the Sunderbans. He described low swampy islands, and vegetation chiefly made up of dwarf-palm trees and small mangroves. Once he sailed up the River Hoogly, he saw taller trees on the riverbanks as well as villages and signs of cultivation.

He rode his first *palki* on the way towards Burdwan in the north, along the Grand Trunk Road. The novelty of the ride was initially pleasing. He marvelled at the neatness with which everything was packed, the good-humoured bearers, the warmth inside when the sliding doors were shut and the breeze when they were open.

The discomforts, however, could be wearisome. The bearers could be greedy and thought nothing of breaking one's sleep by insisting on *baksheesh* (tips) whenever a change of shift happened and a new set of bearers took over. The dust and stifling heat also got to him. By the end of it all, he was left with aching bones and a giddy head.

The raja of Burdwan (in Bengal), his host for a brief while, had immense grounds where Hooker had his first glimpse of 'oriental gardening', as he termed the gardens of the east. Small mud paths ran through rice fields, bordered with bamboo, jackfruit, casuarina, and chinaberry trees. Tanks were prominent features, full of lilies, and fringed by palm and date trees. Hooker was obviously meticulous about noting such things. The king also had a menagerie where Hooker saw two kangaroos, the female with her young in her pouch.

The Dangers of India

The river between Benares and Calcutta was full of gangs of robbers called 'thugs', Hooker wrote, who sailed in crews of fifteen in as many as 250 boats. They preyed on the pilgrim traffic, offering conveyance to those unwary and ignorant. At a given signal the crews

An Elephant Ride

An elephant ride provided yet another new experience. He found his own elephant docile, obedient and very clever too. Seated high up meant he was away from the dust, though the constant swinging motion proved nauseating. The mahout, or driver, guided the elephant by poking his big toe under either ear, or sometimes ensured obedience with an iron goad, hammering the poor animal's head with some force. But the elephant was so cooperative that he would pick up pieces of stone, and with a jerk of his trunk throw them over his head for the rider to catch, thus saving Hooker the trouble of dismounting to 'geologize'!

rushed in, doubled up on the chosen victim, strangled him with silk kerchiefs and, having robbed him, threw him into the river, where floating corpses were often too numerous to elicit even a sad exclamation.

It would be another few years before the British soldier, William Henry Sleeman, and his band of Indian informants, tracked down the *thuggie* hideouts and eliminated the danger they posed.

To Hooker, the astronomical observatory was the most interesting place in Benares, though it was by then dirty and ruinous. Its great stone instruments were in a state of decay. The square-shaped building had a central court and flat roof, around which the astrolabes and other instruments were arranged. The astronomer-royal, who showed Hooker around, appeared pitiful and confessed to Hooker that he was very hungry. The observatory was supported by the king of Jaipur, who paid him a scanty pittance.

Mirzapore (now Mirzapur) was his last stop in the plains before he headed up to Darjeeling. He described it as a straggling town, with about 100,000 inhabitants. The town, to him, offered a mix of squalor and gaudiness. It had large squares and broad streets, and then, acres of low huts and groves of trees. The Ganga flowed nearby, and the numerous fine trees along its banks made the town pleasing in many ways.

Mirzapore was known for its carpet-weaving. It was also a mart for indigo seeds from Bundelkhand, and cotton, lac, sugar and saltpetre (potassium nitrate). Other native industries included brassware and idols made of sandstone.

From Mirzapore, Hooker took a boat to travel down the Ganga towards Darjeeling. On the way, he stopped at Patna and visited its famous opium factory, about which he had been curious. The vessel he sailed on was slow and shabby, but it was spacious, measuring 40 by 30 feet. It looked like a floating haystack, or even a thatched cottage. His living quarters, neatly framed with matting and quite like a house, lay on the deck.

The Diwan of Darjeeling

Darjeeling had been given to the British by the king of Sikkim. It was now a much-needed sanatorium for

British soldiers, and a place of respite for their families. Its temperate climate and nearness to Calcutta were added attractions.

It was with the succession of a new king that friction developed between British India and Sikkim. The *diwan* of Sikkim was of Tibetan origin and rumoured to be pro-Chinese, and close to the Nepalese. He also happened to be a relative of Sikkim's queen. Hooker described him as an insolent and greedy man, who tried to monopolize the trade of the country and enrich himself with taxes levied on British goods.

The *diwan* tried in every manner possible to prevent an amicable understanding between Sikkim and the British government. Hooker, whose loyalties were clearly British, wrote in his notes about how every friendly British offer was turned down. Not only did Sikkim tax British goods 'more', but it also offered shelter to notorious offenders and fugitives from law, and many a time, messengers sent by the British Indian government were arbitrarily taken captive. Diplomatic patience on the part of the British government at Calcutta was misread as weakness and timidity.

Making Friends in Darjeeling

Darjeeling, despite this tension, had seen a rapid rise in population – of soldiers and their families, and Indians from elsewhere who came to serve this growing populace. There was also considerable trade in musk, salt, gold dust, borax, woollen cloth, and especially ponies brought down from Tibet. Trade had been improved by the annual fair that Dr Archibald Campbell, the British superintendent in Darjeeling, introduced right at the foot of the hills, which drew buyers and sellers alike.

Dr Campbell also accompanied Hooker on his journey north towards the Kanchenjunga and the passes that led to Tibet. Brian Hodgson, scholar, and once resident at the royal court of Nepal, was often Hooker's host as well. Hooker was greatly inspired by him. He described Hodgson as a devoted, tireless scholar, interested in knowledge for its own sake. Hodgson had studied Buddhism and painstakingly chronicled the languages, customs and faiths of the many ethnic groups in the eastern Himalayan foothills. The valuable knowledge base Hodgson had built up about Nepal, its languages, flora and fauna made him aptly deserving of the title – 'father of Himalayan studies'.

The Magic of the Mountains

Kanchenjunga was about 60 kilometres away from Darjeeling district, rising over 21,000 feet, far above wooded hills, and the River Rangeet appeared, as Hooker wrote, like a silver line with clouds of foam. Hooker found the Himalayan peaks more beautiful than the Swiss Alps. He noted the precision and sharpness of their outlines, and the wonderful play of colours on the snowy flanks. The sinking or rising sun painted the clouds in shades of orange, gold and ruby, and twilight presented an awesome spectacle as the red tinge slowly gave place to an emerald green.

HOOKER IN THE HIMALAYAN MOUNTAINS

The Naming Game

The Siniolchu peak in Sikkim made for a favourite excursion spot from Darjeeling. The route to it, Hooker noted, was full of rare and beautiful plants. Hooker and Campbell, with their Lepcha guides (who belonged to an ethnic group native to these parts), passed through magnificent forests of oak, magnolia and rhododendron, and the summit presented a grand view of Darjeeling and beyond.

The white-flowered magnolia was the predominant tree at heights of 7,000 to 8,000 feet. As Hooker passed through, he saw that the trees bore profuse blossoms and the forests on the mountain flanks appeared sprinkled with snow. The purple-flowered magnolia, which he named after his friend, put forth, during the flowering season, great rose-purple cup-shaped flowers, whose fleshy petals covered the ground pleasingly.

On the branches of this tree, and others like the oak and laurel tree, the *Rhododendron dalhousiæ* thrived. It was a slender shrub and bore white lemon-scented bells at the end of each branch. He also noted the scarlet rhododendron and the *Rhododendron argenteum* that could grow as high as a 40-foot tree, with magnificent leaves and white flowers growing in clusters. There were also a variety of ferns that grew in these forests.

The further they progressed, the more entrancing was the natural beauty around them. Once they advanced deeper into Sikkim, however, things became more and more dangerous.

Villages on the hillside sometimes burnt tracts of forestland for cultivation. The forests, dry and full of bamboo, extending over steep hills, sometimes appeared like a blazing spectacle, as the fire took hold. Heavy clouds shut out the entire sky; and everything in the air around, even the birds and insects, seemed

RHODODENDRON DALHOUSIAE

RHODODENDRON ARGENTEUM

hushed. Only the harsh roar of the rivers rose above the sound of crackling wood.

Going up to the Border

Close to the border, once they were about to enter the passes into Tibet, Hooker and Campbell were delayed for a while when their guides did not turn up. After a while, part of a wedding procession came up. The bridegroom, a handsome young Lepcha, led cattle intended for the feast. The group volunteered to help them. On the flatlands by the stream grew the sago palm, which grew 10 feet high with a beautiful crown of foliage.

Hooker was also struck by the amazing number of spectacular butterflies, especially the large tropical 'swallowtails', black in colour with wings that had scarlet or yellow eyes. They appeared to sail majestically through the still hot air, or fluttered from one rock to another, and often settled on the damp sand by the river. This reminded him, as Hooker evocatively described, of a crowded fleet of yachts on a calm day.

Cane-bridges, simply made, dilapidated yet hardy, helped them cross the rapid streams and rivulets on the way. In places, the bamboo plant grew in abundance. The great bamboo grew to a height of 40 to 60 feet, its leaves largely used for making houses.

There were nearly a dozen kinds of bamboo. The young shoots of several were edible, while the seeds of one were often made into a fermented drink and into bread in times of scarcity.

THE HIMALAYAN LANDSCAPE

The Handy Bamboo

The bamboo came in handy when a house had to be quickly constructed, as happened when Hooker and Campbell were caught in an unexpected downpour. Their guides cut down strips of bamboo to form posts, quickly made a thatched roof using bamboo and the broad leaves of the wild plantain. They came up with a table of four posts, using cross pieces of wood, lashed with strips of bamboo. More stalks of bamboo were cut and flattened to form a bed or a chair. In just about an hour, half a dozen men, using only long knives, put up a tolerably watertight furnished house. A thick flooring of bamboo leaves kept the feet dry, and a screen of bamboo and other foliage from all around made the small house reasonably warm.

Trouble at Tumlong

At Tonglu, the view was spectacular. Hooker had a good view of the Himalayas, with Sikkim on the right, Nepal on the left and the plains of India to the south. In the early morning, the transparency of the atmosphere granted an astonishing grandeur to the view. Kanchenjunga to the north appeared a dazzling mass of snowy peaks, intersected by blue glaciers that gleamed in the slanting rays of the rising sun, like, as he wrote, 'aquamarine stones set in frosted silver'.

Trouble caught up with them once they passed through the Donkia Pass (now Dongkha La) in November 1849. As they tried to cross into Tibet, a band of Sikkimese guards arrested them and forced them to come back to Tumlong in north Sikkim. Campbell was handcuffed and singled out for harsh treatment. Once in Tumlong, he was beaten up and imprisoned in a cell underneath the ruler's palace.

A tenuous treaty, somewhat 'vague' in its terms, then existed between Sikkim and the British, and the *diwan*, more favourably inclined towards the Tibetans and Chinese, took full advantage of this. The *diwan* and the faction he controlled wanted to use the hostages as bargaining chips, hoping the British Indian government would agree to a more beneficial treaty, giving them more concessions.

Hooker kept his presence of mind and continued looking for plants, making his notes even in the period of his incarceration. He made an enormous collection of seeds, gathering dozens of rhododendron species from the nearby Lagyap valley, many of which still survive in British and Irish gardens. One of Hooker's finest discoveries, just before his arrest, was the *Rhododendron niveum* that he found in places just east of Tumlong. Today this is one of the rarest rhododendron species in the Himalayas. The best place to see it today is in the Yumthang Valley (the Sikkim Valley of Flowers sanctuary). In May every year, the plant bears densely packed flowers in shades of magenta and purple. Hooker introduced this intriguing species to broader cultivation and it is today the state tree of Sikkim.

The Diwan Eats Humble Pie

Campbell and Hooker were accused of having entered the country without approval from the authorities and against the will of the Raja of Sikkim. Campbell was singled out because he had earlier meted out harsh fines to many for breaking laws, and they were now among his chief tormentors. The *diwan* claimed the king was under no obligation to the East India Company that was then in control of large parts of India.

The *diwan* arrived at Tumlong, but he dithered about a formal meeting with Hooker. The oldest and most venerated lama from the Pemayangtse Monastery in north-eastern Sikkim travelled to Tumlong, hoping to intercede and secure their immediate release. A faction in the Sikkim court favouring a compromise with the British had reached out to the lama. These negotiations, and fear of reprisal from Calcutta, the seat of British Indian administration then, led to Hooker and

Campbell's release on 7 December 1849. It was speeded up when news came that a 'sepoy regiment' was on its way from Calcutta to Sikkim. The king and queen sent costly parting gifts as an apology and reparation. As a result of this famous hostage crisis, the government in Calcutta annexed the lower half of Sikkim, bringing it under the direct control of British India.

Hooker was the first European to collect plants in this area and he discovered more than twenty species of Himalayan rhododendrons. His discoveries remain important to understanding botanical evolution and how plants adapt to varying environmental conditions.

But there was more to Hooker than this. He later worked with Charles Darwin to classify plants the latter had collected in the Galapagos Islands (South America), and their collaboration remains famous in the history of botany. An illustration discovered a century later also established that Joseph Dalton Hooker was the first western visitor to sketch Mount Everest. This work dated to 1848 and was found among Hooker's papers in the Royal Botanic Gardens at Kew, where Hooker was director in the late nineteenth century, succeeding his father.

5

THE SEARCH FOR A MAGICAL PLANT

CLEMENTS MARKHAM GOES FAR SOUTH

What on earth could a Spanish countess have to do with a herb that was said to cure a mosquito-borne disease on the Indian subcontinent?

For centuries, a unique plant had grown in the hilly region of Peru, a country in north-western South America. Tall and evergreen, with tapering oval leaves and pinkish-white flowers, the plant was highly valued because of its bark. The native groups who had lived there for long knew that its bark, once stripped, crushed and made edible by boiling it along with additives like rose-leaf and clove, could be a cure for many illnesses, especially malaria.

The tree's value increased with the arrival of the Spanish as conquerors and missionaries.

The story goes how in the 1660s a Spanish countess suffering from fever and chills – all symptoms of malaria – was miraculously cured when her husband, then viceroy of Peru, gave her a concoction to drink. It was made from the bark of a tree, mixed with herbs like clove to disguise its bitterness. The countess recovered, and the tree, giver of the life-saving medicine, was given her name – Cinchona. But, in fact, this magical, all-curing plant with its medicinal properties had been known to the local people for centuries.

The arrival of the Spanish in South America set off a rush for the bark. Explorers from rival nations began making secret expeditions, hoping to evade the Spanish who held this territory, and demanded a high price for it. Seekers and adventurers journeyed deep into the rainforests, hoping to strip the bark from the tree.

The search was complicated because not all species of the cinchona tree were effective. The Dutch were the first to try and cultivate the tree in Indonesia, their colony in the East. But this failed because the wrong species had been grown.

In the 1820s, French chemists identified two of the principal alkaloids present in the bark, called quinine and cinchonine. So it was easier to isolate these from the bark, rather than pulling the tree apart, which had been the earlier method of extraction.

An Early Adventurer

A British man, Clements Markham, was one of many adventurers who set out to find the cinchona plant. He was born in 1830 in Yorkshire in west England, to a relatively privileged family. His father was a clergyman, appointed to a high position in Windsor Castle, one of the royal homes, and Clements's maternal grandfather was a baronet. Clements was always fond of reading adventure stories as a young boy, and history was a subject that especially fascinated him.

He wrote his own concise history of England when he was ten. His father, a clergyman, had a small printing press to produce his own parish notices, so he published copies of Clements's book. In another year, he had moved on – this time writing about the peoples of the world. He drew his own rough maps too.

It was a time when scientific explorations began to be made in earnest, and adventurers, geographers and others travelled to lands considered 'mysterious' and 'unknown' like the East or even the interiors of continents like Africa and America. As you know, this exploration led to many discoveries, but also the exploitation of people there, along with their resources.

Markham, though he believed in the superiority of the West, was driven by his love for adventure and his desire to see as much of the world as possible.

CLEMENTS MARKHAM AS A YOUNG NAVAL CADET

Young Clements impressed the admiral of the British Royal Navy with his desire to travel, to voyage on seas and explore new lands, and so his naval career began early. He joined as a cadet, but his social connections ensured that he had good sleeping quarters and ate well, and so he never did have too rough a voyage.

Headed to Antarctica

He sailed in the HMS *Collingwood* towards Antarctica in 1844. He spent months in Chile in South America, and then in the islands of Tahiti in the Pacific Ocean. Here, his sympathies were with the rebels who were fighting the French royal forces. It was this sympathy for the underdog or the powerless that soon left him disillusioned with the Royal Navy. He noted how crewmen were punished harshly, even flogged, for the smallest error. However, he was persuaded by his father to stay on in the navy for a bit.

He travelled with another mission in search of the lost expedition of John Franklin, the British explorer.

HMS *COLLINGWOOD*, THE SHIP ON WHICH MARKHAM SAILED TO SOUTH AMERICA

Franklin and his crew in four ships had not returned after they had gone in search of a northern route to Asia, sailing from the Atlantic Ocean, through the cold icy sea passages of the Arctic region, to the Pacific Ocean. It was believed the ships had floundered in the frozen, ice-filled waters, and the men had perished due to the cold and the lack of food. Yet their remains would not be found until after a century.

Two years later, in 1852, aided by a little financial assistance from his father, the adventure-seeking Markham joined an expedition to Peru. Drawn by memories of his first expedition to South America, he was very enthusiastic.

The Charms of Peru

This time, his ship sailed first across the Atlantic Ocean to the east Canadian coast of Nova Scotia. Then, he travelled by land to Boston and New York, and sailed on to Panama. Having crossed the small isthmus (in those days, the Panama Canal hadn't yet been built), his ship brought him to Peru in October. The journey took two months in all.

He stopped first at Ayacucho on the Peruvian coast, along the Pacific Ocean. It had been the site of a famous battle, when Simon Bolivar, 'the liberator' (of several countries in South America), had led his armies to victory against the 'royalists' who represented and supported the Spanish conquerors. The city had been inhabited for a thousand years and more, especially from the time of the Incas, a civilization known for its cleverly built cities that still survive. Markham stayed here till December.

Then he left for Cuzco, a town across the Andes Mountains. He was especially fascinated by the Quechua people who lived here. The Quechua language had once been spoken by the Incas and it is still spoken all along the west coast of South America.

This journey involved the precarious crossing of a river called the Apurimac that ran through steep narrow gorges, its flow punctuated by many rapids. A bridge made of grass-ropes swung in the wind, and yet proved durable. Markham remained in the city for about six months, drawn by its language and its old buildings, some still standing. It was during his travels here and to neighbouring areas that Markham first heard of the cinchona tree and its amazing properties. He had no idea then that he would return to this area barely six years later in 1859, with a clear mission in mind: to get seeds of this coveted tree, to ensure that these could be planted in India for an assured and continuous supply.

Mission Cinchona in Peru

By this time, Markham had begun working in the India Office, the headquarters in London, first of the East India Company, and then the British Crown that took over administration of India following the uprising of 1857.

To maintain control and prevent more such conflicts, the British administration understood the need to raise the efficiency and morale of its soldiers, most of whom were Indians. It was critical to raise mortality levels, and since malaria – its cause was still unclear then – claimed many lives at this time, the government realized the value of cinchona. Recommendations had been made since the 1810s to grow cinchona in the Nilgiri hills of south India, where conditions were similar to Peru, but only after 1857 was this matter taken up with urgency.

Clements Markham, on account of his high position – he was now a 'geographer' in the India Office – and his familiarity with Peru, was chosen to lead the expedition. It promised to be quite an adventure. The cinchona trees were zealously guarded. Markham also knew he had to look for a particular species of cinchona tree, one that would prove 'febrifugal' – that is, fever-reducing and bitter-tasting – and they had to hunt for it stealthily and secretly.

Expeditions were arduous and required intense preparations. Voyagers were going into the unknown, quite like space voyages today! There was no air-conditioning, no refrigeration, and food had to be safely packaged: smoked, salted or pickled or else stored in cool, dry containers or storerooms.

Markham's ship set off in 1859. His earlier visit to Cuzco had made him familiar with the area's history. He also knew a bit of the language. The entire expedition took three years. The cinchona they were looking for was deep in the forests of Tambopata in Caravaya province.

Going up the Andes

The search began with days of strenuous climbing. They walked through forests and grassy highlands, and climbed steep mountains till the rivers far below appeared like glittering ribbons. The ultimate object of their arduous hunt was a particular species of cinchona shrub – the Calisaya shrub.

The thick forests could get dark, even in the day! The team often found shelter in bamboo huts left by earlier travellers – like a team from Bolivia that had come in search of incense.

A bit further on, Markham's group came upon a small farm managed by an eccentric old Bolivian who cultivated corn and sugar, and had a makeshift distillery to make rum as well. He used primitive tools, but his knowledge of the weather and soil and other natural conditions impressed Markham. He valued the knowledge that the local people possessed and this helped his explorations.

They made careful preparations to set off for the more difficult part of their journey, paying attention to the clothes and the provisions needed.

This part of the forested area was rarely traversed. Markham's party of seven included three from native Peruvian tribes, who knew the area; Mariano Martinez and Pablo Sevallos, two mestizos, that is, men of mixed ancestry (maybe Peruvian-Spaniard), who were especially knowledgeable about local customs and laws; and a botanical expert simply called Weir.

The local men had their *chuspas* (pouches) of cocoa and a *chumpi* or belt round their waists, and they carried the provisions. Pablo managed the tent, and everyone else was armed with machetes, or wood-knives, to clear the way. They were dressed in coarse cotton cloth, and

CINCHONA CALISAYA

The Healers of the Jungle

Early in May, as they trudged into the forest, half a dozen pale-faced men unexpectedly emerged from the tangled thicket in front. They looked, as Markham described, wan and cadaverous, like men risen from the dead, and worn out by long walking and fatigue. They turned out to be 'Collahuayas', collectors of drugs and incense, who penetrated deep into the forests to obtain their wares, and often looked pale and haggard.

The Collahuayas originally lived in three villages in the forest-covered ravines of northern South America. Their knowledge of herbs was passed on from one generation to the next since time immemorial. They travelled through the forests, collecting herbs and vital specimens, before setting out as healers to faraway parts, staying away from home for two or three years.

Dressed in black breeches, red ponchos and broad-brimmed hats, they carried boxes of medicines on their backs. Clements described their methods in the book he wrote later. Their treatment involved purging or puncturing the body to let out the poisoned blood. They administered the powdered leaf of the *sayri* (tobacco) for headaches, *mulli* (*Schinus molle*) for wounds and a host of other herbs for various ailments.

Markham wore a leather hat, red woollen shirt, fustian trousers and the indispensable *polccos*, or shoes made of 'wool felt', always used in these forests.

A River and Its Dangers

The really serious forest work for Markham and his team began once they were beyond the River Challuma (Yacuma) in western Peru. The Andes Mountains lay just ahead. There was no road at all, and the team cut its way through the bushes. Trees towered over them and the ground was swamped with creepers, fallen masses of tangled bamboo, and long tendrils that could twist around the ankles and trip the unwary traveller.

In places, they moved along dense forests, right on the verge of giddy precipices that overlooked the river. They struggled on until sunset, when they reached a stone-filled area along the riverbank and camped for the night. The pattern was repeated over the next several days.

It was a surreal scene every time the darkness closed round them: the campfire on the beach, the dense gloomy forest close behind, the surging river in front and forest-clad mountains rising on the other side.

The Good-Humoured Guides

Markham praised his guide Martinez, who had, over the years, trekked a lot through these forests and could be relied on to spot the Calisaya plant. It required quickness and a keen eye to distinguish between the various species amid the dense undergrowth and thick forests. Martinez had a thorough knowledge of forest lore, loved woodcraft, and was acquainted with the native name of almost every plant, and the value and uses these had.

At dawn, the guides found the marks of a jaguar on the beach close to the tent, and a huge snake wriggled through the fallen trees as they re-entered the forest. The brilliant colours and great variety of butterflies were striking.

One particular species caught Markham's eye: it had bright blue and crimson wings, its underside marked by a clear pattern of dark lines, as if drawn by a sharp quill, on a snow-white ground, edged with deep blue. Soon they came to the foot of a tremendous precipice, which Martinez called Casa-sani. It was edged with rocks, and the river flowed narrowly through. The cinchona region was rumoured to be close.

They ascended the western precipice by a precarious ladder, naturally formed of ledge-like notches in the rock, or half-rotten branches of trees. The summit, though, presented a glorious view of forest-covered mountains, running up into sharp peaks, with graceful palms towering above the other trees and standing out against the sky. Several Calisaya-trees seemed to be growing on the summit, with clearly noticeable bunches of seeds as well as seedlings.

Despite the dangers, the magnitude and variety of the trees of the forest were breathtaking. The imposing character of the scenery was a source of joy and lightened the fatigue of the journey.

Getting Over a Scare

They attempted to wade across the River Tambopata but found the current too strong. They camped that night on an island, on the river's left bank. After sunset it rained heavily, and the waters rose through the night. Markham feared the island where they had camped would soon be submerged, and indeed the river came to within a few feet of his tent.

The next day, he tried to cross the river again, hoping to ford it at several points with a long pole as support. But the water was deep, swollen and very rapid, and Markham was nearly carried away by a strong current. They hastily moved their camp to another narrow part of the beach overshadowed by the forest. It was the point where the muddy waters of a smaller river, the Yanamayu, met the Tambopata.

Finding the Cinchona

They ascended from the north-eastern side of the Yanamayu, where, at a height of 450 feet, there was a level bit of land covered with palms and bamboo. Their search was chiefly conducted along a ridge above this plateau, where the bamboo forests ended.

That day, they had an early success, as they obtained some plants of the cinchona species they had come in search of. Markham reported seeing a couple of *tunquis*, birds with the most gorgeous plumage he had ever seen. They were like large pigeons, with orange-scarlet feathers on the head, neck, breast and tail, black wings, a light-grey back, and a bright red crest. The butterflies and moths were numerous and brilliant, but so tame, and in such swarms, as to be a perfect plague.

There was one bright swallowtail, with blue wings fringed with crimson. Yet the torment inflicted by venomous insects was maddening; especially from a kind of fly which in a moment raised swellings and blood-red lumps all over the hands and face, causing pain and irritation. Every evening, it rained heavily, making the river water surge ominously.

MARKHAM AS A YOUNG MAN

The collection of cinchona plants was deposited in a shady place near the tent, the roots being well covered over with soft moss.

In the Towering Forests

Markham was still keen to explore the right bank of the River Tambopata. To him, it promised to yield more of the cinchona he was looking over. They stayed back for another day. He once almost put his hand on a viper and came across two bears sunning themselves by the precipice.

In this part of the jungle, the trees rose high, growing almost 50 or 60 feet from the ground. The inner bark of some of these trees had a strong taste of cinnamon, and it was used to scent and flavour the *huarapu*, or fermented sugar-cane juice. On many trees there were immense heaps or clods of earth, called *cotocuro*, growing right on the trunk. These heaps of soil, like small hills, grew huge over the centuries – sometimes eight to 10 feet high, and three or four feet across – and were made by teams of small yellowish lice that Markham spotted swarming between each layer.

On 7 May, they awoke to find that their food supplies had dipped alarmingly, and it was necessary to beat a hasty retreat. The plants were carefully packed in layers of moss and sewn up in two bundles of thick matted cloth. In all, they had gathered about 400 cinchona plants.

Threats and Warnings

As Markham and his team were about to set off for the journey homeward, an ominous letter came from Don José Mariano Bobadilla, the municipal head of Quiaca (in Sandia province of south-west Peru), forbidding the team from taking away a single plant. Markham and his guides were threatened with arrest. Though Markham responded with his own indignant letter, he knew they had to make a quick escape. A posse of local policemen was coming down the valley to seize him and destroy their collection of cinchona plants.

Early on the morning of 12 May 1860, he took leave of the honest forester Martinez who had assisted them. Markham hoped he would not suffer for helping them. As Markham wrote that the 'melancholiest part of travelling is the parting with friends, never to meet again'.

On arriving at Sandia, he paid off his guides. Markham wrote of how willing, hard-working, intelligent, helpful, and good-humoured they were, quick in setting up encampments, conversing quietly and treating animals with kindness.

Making a Quick Getaway

At Sandia though, things were in an alarming state. He encountered several officials determined to prevent him from continuing his journey with the cinchona plants.

Markham was stopped from hiring mules to carry his goods, and he had no option but to head for the city of Crucero. He feared the plants would be killed by the frost there. In despair, he considered setting out on foot, with all four bundles of plants on his own mule, when a municipal officer, Don Manuel Mena, came to his help.

This official took him aside and told him that if Markham would gift him his gun, he would get a local man to supply more mules to carry loads, and there would also be someone to accompany him to Vilque, on the road to Arequipa, the port city. Clements willingly agreed to this bargain and then took a less frequented route, staying out of sight of more officials, to reach the port city.

Still, the difficulties of getting the plants out of the country were not over. The superintendent of the

A SCENE OF AREQUIPA

custom house of Islay refused to allow the plants to be shipped without a special order from the minister of finance and commerce at Lima, the nation's capital. So Markham travelled to Lima to obtain the order from the minister. He returned with it to Islay on 23 June.

That evening, the cases were placed on a small launch, ready to go on board the steamer the next morning. But at night, attempts were made to bribe the man in charge to bore holes and kill the plants by pouring in boiling water, but fortunately this devious plan failed. The plants were carefully guarded and, the following day, they were safely lodged on the steamer bound for Panama.

Markham regretted that the plants had not been taken directly to India, that is, right from Panama on a ship across the Pacific. Most of them would have then arrived in perfect condition in Madras. Instead, the plants went through a long voyage and then an arduous overland journey as well.

The Journey of the Plants

Two months later, the plants arrived in England, in August, still flourishing and healthy, and remained so until their arrival at Alexandria, in Egypt, early in September. The intense heat of the Red Sea, however, where the temperatures always ranged in the high 40°C, proved too much for them, and the damage was increased by a detention of a week at Bombay (now Mumbai). They were already affected by the intense heat of the Red Sea and the Arabian Sea, and it was a while before the plants reached their final destination in south India, where they were supposed to be replanted.

Following Markham's lead, there were two other expeditions – Richard Spruce went to Ecuador for the red-bark cinchona and another botanical expert called Ward returned with the 'grey-bark' cinchona. The plants they gathered came to India via different routes. Unfortunately, most of the seedlings brought by Markham did not survive the tropical heat when the ship sailed through the Red Sea. But others he had collected, which were shipped later in colder months, did survive. These plants were also transported in the sturdier and better-made 'Wardian' cases (terrarium containers of wood with glass fronts, designed to carry plants). These were like small, portable greenhouses that helped regulate heat.

Despite the mixed results of his own expedition, Markham always believed that an exchange of products between old and new worlds helped humankind in general. He insisted that with sustained cultivation of cinchona in India and Java, its world's supply would increase, and it would help Peru restore its own production of the precious plant, which had been hunted and chopped down recklessly over the years.

Later in life, Clements Markham became associated with the Royal Geographical Society in the UK, serving as its secretary for twenty-five years and then as president for another twelve. He remained ever encouraging of other explorers, especially those headed to unknown regions like the South Pole.

6

TRAVELS TO THE FORBIDDEN CITY

NAIN SINGH IN LHASA

The first ever detailed mapping of the Himalayas and the famous Great Trigonometrical Survey could not have taken place without this brave and daring man.

In the mid-nineteenth century, the map of British India showed a large swathe of land north of the Himalayas. This was Tibet, a chilly, mysterious and desolate kingdom that shared a border with India right from Kashmir and Ladakh across Nepal, and far to the east.

Tibet was cold. A land of craggy peaks and vast expanses of tabletop plateaus, covered with ice in winters and tall dry grass in warmer seasons. As forbidding fortresses of stone gazed down from heights, it was a place where for long distances the traveller saw nothing before coming upon a caravan of people on yaks and small ponies, the sound of their bells and the sweeping wind often the only sounds heard for days, even weeks. The Himalayas that acted as Tibet's natural boundary wall with British India to the south were marked by long ranges, high peaks, deep crevices, and sweeping glaciers that gave rise to mighty rivers like the Ganga, the Brahmaputra and the Indus.

British interest in Tibet came from several factors. It was the age of exploration, of new advances in cartography, and so mountaineers, surveyors and explorers travelled far, some on their own, some engaged by the government to survey and map unexplored, unknown places.

Tibet was also important strategically. For centuries, traders and travellers had journeyed to and from Tibet via the passes that Nature had carved through the mountains. There was also regular pilgrim traffic to the holy monasteries and sacred places nestled in the ranges. A more accurate knowledge of the passes, where these led, and the 'secret' cities and villages that lay on the way would add to British India's knowledge of the countries that lay beyond: not just Tibet, but China and Russia as well.

Lands North

The British wanted control not only of areas that bordered Tibet, like Sikkim and Nepal, and to the north, Ladakh and Kashmir (semi-independent kingdoms at the time), but also knowledge of these areas – the routes, the terrain, the people who lived there, the languages they spoke, the goods they traded in, and the natural riches like minerals and plants that were available.

The fear of a slowly advancing Russia in the north-west also added an urgency to the British intentions. Russia was a big power, and like other powerful European empires like France and Germany, it too was interested in extending its influence over other regions: for resources, and the prestige that was attached to conquest then.

The Surveyors and Their Plans

In 1802, when the British began their great surveying exercise to map the peaks, the passes and the true extent of the Himalayas – called the Great Trigonometrical Survey – they had to be careful, especially in the north. Strangers were looked upon with suspicion and regarded as spies. Their lives were often endangered if they took on openly risky missions.

So, from 1860 onward, the British explorers hit on a strategy: to reach out to those local traders from Kumaon and the regions in the lower Himalayas who travelled to Tibet often and knew the routes and stops well. It was, the British thought, not a risk to plant a surveyor in their midst. Someone who looked like a trader, even a pilgrim, who spoke the language, was discreet and knowledgeable, and could mingle easily with the caravans headed to Tibet.

NAIN SINGH RAWAT

Nain Singh Rawat fit the bill in every way.

The Travelling Bhotias

A British surveyor, Captain Thomas Montgomerie, picked Nain Singh Rawat, who had glowing recommendations from those who knew him and Montgomerie's juniors. Montgomerie was impressed by Nain Singh's intelligence, discretion and ability to follow instructions – something that mattered to his British superiors.

Nain Singh was from the Bhotia ethnic group. His village, Milam, was in the Johar Valley, at the foot of the Gori Ganga glacier and close to the Nanda Devi peak in present-day Uttarakhand. The Bhotias had historic trading ties with Tibet. They were the only people allowed in to trade by the Tibetan authorities of Nari-Khorsum (in Ngari prefecture, the part of Tibet in the basin of the upper River Sutlej, and north of Kumaon and Garhwal).

Every summer, when the snow melted, the Bhotias moved across the passes that linked Ladakh and Kumaon to Tibet. In winter, when the freeze set in, they moved lower down to the Indian plains, travelling to major towns like Simla (Shimla), Benares (Varanasi), Patna, and even on occasion, Calcutta. They brought with them the produce of Tibet (salt, borax, wool, gold dust and also ponies) while Tibet for its part needed grain of all kinds, especially rice (as not much grain was grown there on account of its high altitude and scarcity of water). The goods were carried on the backs of sheep, goats, ponies, yaks and *jhoopoos* (a cross between the Tibetan yak and the hill cow).

Special Arrangements for a Pilgrim

Nain Singh was to go as a pilgrim, dressed in a monk's robes and carrying with him a pilgrim's artefacts: rosary beads and a Tibetan prayer wheel. The hundred rosary beads (not the usual one hundred and eight that sacred rosaries had) helped him measure distance, and the prayer wheel, placed securely inside its octangular box over a cylinder-like tube, contained his notes and instructions.

When people came up to Nain Singh, the sight of his prayer wheel was sufficient to prevent them from addressing him. They thought that he was absorbed in religious contemplation.

Nain Singh also carried a thermometer to measure temperature when he boiled water at different altitudes, along with other instruments, like the sextant to record latitude and a compass hidden away. He also had a wooden bowl like the ones carried at the waist by all Bhotias. It was used for drinking, whether water, tea, broth, or even spirits.

Up North from Kathmandu

For their first mission, Montgomerie wanted Nain and his cousin Mani Singh Rawat to survey the road starting from Gartok, the town in Tibet closest to

Ladakh, to follow it south-east towards the holy lake of Mansarovar, and beyond for several hundred miles toward Lhasa, the Tibetan capital. This road, known as a major trading route between Ladakh and Lhasa, also followed the River Tsangpo, which later became the Brahmaputra when it entered India. Besides information about the route, they had to gather as much knowledge as they could about Lhasa, which was known as 'the forbidden city'. No one then really knew where exactly Lhasa was located; the little that was known was based on conjecture gathered from travellers.

Nain Singh, born in 1830, was a schoolteacher before he was selected for service. The prefix 'Pandit' attached to his name, as a teacher, soon came to denote other surveyors like him.

In 1865, Nain Singh and his cousin, Mani Singh, set off on their expedition. The perils and challenges they faced, Nain Singh in particular, can be gleaned from survey reports that were compiled and later translated into English. It was hard for the cousins to join the trade caravans travelling from Kumaon. They had travelled for trade before and now feared they would be too easily recognized at the border posts. They decided then to move eastward to Kathmandu, in Nepal, and trace their way up north towards Tibet, again by joining a trade caravan while pretending to be pilgrims.

A Suspicious Governor

They reached Kathmandu on 7 March 1865. From here, they planned to head to the town of Kerun Shahr (now

Gyirong Town) in south Tibet. They started on 20 March with great hopes, accompanied by four men hired to be their helpers.

Six days later, they stopped at a village, where they changed their attire to appear as merchants. At every stop, however, they were accosted by custom officials who checked their equipment thoroughly. They were suspicious, for already other explorers had tried to reach Lhasa by hook or by crook.

Days later, a message from the governor at Gyirong reached them at Paimunesa on the banks of the River Gandak, forbidding them from continuing the journey. Officials were suspicious of them because they had not taken the preferred, somewhat easier, route to Lhasa, the one via the Kumaon passes. So they had no option but to turn back to Kathmandu.

Moreover, they soon learnt that the Kerun Shahr governor was well acquainted with Pandit Mani Singh when the former had been posted elsewhere. There was no way now the cousins could fool him, and Nain Singh knew he had to go ahead alone and try something else to succeed in his mission.

A Laid-back Merchant

Back in Kathmandu, Nain Singh heard that a Bhotia merchant was travelling to Lhasa via Kerun Shahr. This merchant, called Dawa Nangal, promised to take Nain Singh to Lhasa, and on the strength of his word, proceeded to borrow money from him. Dawa Nangal, however, kept delaying the day of their departure.

At long last, Nain Singh set off alone with one of the merchant's helpers. Nain Singh now wore the traditional long robe of a Ladakhi and sported a pigtail. They left Kathmandu on 3 June and reached Shabru on 20 June, where he received unexpected help from Dawa Nangal's family.

Dawa Nangal's uncle was a man of some authority in the area. Quite in sympathy with Nain Singh, the uncle gave him a pass to Kerun Shahr as well as a letter to Dawa Nangal's brother, who had just returned from Lhasa. He assured Nain Singh that Dawa's brother would help arrange his journey to Lhasa and, if necessary, vouch for him before the local officials.

In early July in 1865, Nain Singh finally arrived at Kerun Shahr. It was a small town, with some fifteen to twenty shops run by the Nepalese and Bhotias. It had a fort and a good-sized temple. Rice was imported and salt was exported: this was the staple trade, in fact, between all Tibet and the southern regions. Among the crops grown were wheat, barley, buckwheat (the local *phanpar*) and mustard.

Mapping a Lake

At Kerun Shahr, Nain Singh secured permission to travel onwards to the Tradom Monastery, a well-known halting place on the road between Lhasa and Gartok.

Beyond Kathmandu, the vegetation thinned out and the landscape became barren. Travelling on, he arrived at Babuk village where Nain Singh learnt that in a few days' time, a large trade caravan with 200 yaks intended

Map
ILLUSTRATING THE JOURNEY OF THE PUNDIT NAIN SINGH
through
GREAT TIBET
FROM LADÁKH TO ASSAM
to accompany the Paper
by
Captn. H. Trotter R.E.
GEOGRAPHICAL MILES
ENGLISH MILES
REFERENCES
Chaka — Salt Lake
Chángmá — Northern
Cho — Freshwater Lake
Chu — River
Chumik — Spring
De — District
Gombá or Gonpá — Monastery
Gangri — Snowy Mountain
Lá — Pass
Lhomá — Southern
Sangpo — Large River
Sumdo — Junction of Streams
Thok or Sarká — Gold Fields
The Pundit's route is colored Red
Longitude East from Greenwich
G R E A T
K H O R
N A R I
H O R
S H A N K H O R
Sárá De
Garche Thol
Ting Che Todma
Thok Jalung
Gartokh
Gar
Bachan
Tirthapuri
Mt. Kailas
Darchan
Lake Rakas Tal
Milam
Mariam La
Tanjan
Daksam
Tadum
Niku
Sarka
Chomanku
BRAHMAPUTRA R.
Nakchang Pooted L.
D O K T H O L
N E P A L
KHATMANDHÚ
Singh gi Cho
Niti Pass

NAIN SINGH'S ROUTE
Chargut Cho Lake
Nakchang Gomnak Changma
BRAHMAPUTRA RIVER
SHIGATZE
DARJEELING
JILPAIGURI
SIKKIM
DHUKPA OR DEBA DHARMA
87
88
89
90
91

to start towards Tradom. Having told some members of the party that he was their fellow countryman, he was gladly invited to travel with them. By this time, it was already 25 August and six months had passed since he had first set out.

Once he reached Tradom, Nain Singh feigned sickness, and was accordingly left behind as the caravan set off again. Nain Singh bid his time, looking for news, and in some days, found a good chance of going to Lhasa in the company of a Ladakhi merchant called Lopchak, who had once worked for the king of Kashmir. On 2 October, Nain Singh set off once again. This time he was more hopeful about reaching Lhasa with no more sudden changes in plan.

Twenty days later, they reached Janglache, or Lhatse, which had a fort and a fine monastery right by the River Nianchu, a tributary of the Tsangpo. From this point people and goods were transported by boats to Shigatze, which was a march of five days down the river. Most of Nain Singh's companions took the boat, as this was faster, but he knew he had to survey the land, so he preferred the land route.

The Lama's Three Important Questions

On 29 October, Nain Singh reached Shigatze, a large town where the rivers Yarlung Tsangpo, and Nianchu joined. It was midway between Kathmandu and Lhasa. Staying in a large caravanserai, Nain Singh took to teaching Nepalese shopkeepers a certain method of calculation, called the 'Hindi' (or Indian) method, and it helped him earn a few rupees.

With the Ladakhi group of merchants, Nain Singh travelled to the great Tashilhumpo Monastery, half a mile (1.2 km) south-west of Shigatze. It was surrounded by a wall, a mile in circumference. Many houses and temples were housed within it. The larger temples had gilded spires. The idols within the temples were studded with precious stones, and gold and silver work, and there were about 3,300 priests in the monastery, the chief being the Panchen Lama.

Nain Singh was a bit nervous, for he had heard that the Panchen Lama could look deep into the secrets of all hearts. Still, keeping a bold face, he went with his companions for an audience before the lama. He was greatly relieved to find that the lama was a mere boy of eleven.

The lama sat on a high throne covered with rich silks. He was surrounded by a number of priests, standing reverentially before him. The worshippers uncovered their heads and bowed low, before offering pieces of silk as gifts. The lama blessed them, placing his hand on their heads.

Once they were seated, the Panchen Lama asked only three questions, as he did to every worshipper. 'Is your king well?', 'Is your country prospering?', and 'Are you in good health?'. The priest then placed a small strip of silk around their shoulders and poured a little tea into their cups from a silver kettle. The meeting was then over.

Nain Singh continued with the merchant caravan towards Lhasa. Two months later, in December 1865, they reached the large town of Gyantse on the River Yarlang Tsangpo, which was then frozen, allowing people to walk across it.

They arrived on the last day of the year at a village on Yamdrok Lake. Nain Singh spent two days walking along the lake's perimeter, hoping to measure it. On the second day he was attacked by a band of robbers but escaped by riding away quickly. Nain Singh estimated the lake to be about 45 miles in circumference (or 72 km), and about 2 to 3 miles (4 km) in width. The lake encircled a large island, with low rounded hills. Between the hills and the lake's edge, a village with a small monastery was clearly visible.

They moved on in a north-easterly direction and finally reached Lhasa on 10 January 1866. It had taken Nain Singh over 10 months to make this journey.

At Last, the Forbidden City

Nain Singh rented two rooms in a building. One of the rooms was perfect for observing the stars. He had been there some 10 days when the Lopchak's men (who had waited for Nain Singh to reach) told him they were going to visit the Ganden Monastery and Nain Singh gladly accompanied them. The name Lhasa meant 'the abode or place of gods', and the monasteries around the town were frequently visited by the devout and faithful.

They stopped first at the Sera Monastery, about three miles away. Within its walls, they could see many smaller temples with gilded spires. The idols, like the ones at Shigatze, were studded with gold, silver, and precious stones. On 24 January, they arrived at the Ganden Monastery, located at the top of another low hill. This Monastery was reported to be even wealthier than the one at Shigatze and inhabited by about 3,300 priests. The next day, they returned to Lhasa.

The city of Lhasa was at a height of 11,400 feet. At its centre was a very large monastery. This was surrounded by bazaars and shops, maintained by Lhasan, Kashmiri, Ladakhi, Uzbek and Nepalese merchants. There were numerous tradesmen from China as well.

Nain Singh met the Grand Lama – later called the Dalai Lama – whom he described as a fair and handsome boy of about thirteen. The lama was seated on a throne six feet high. On a lower throne to his right was seated his chief minister, the Gyalbo or Potolah Baja, as he was called by the Nepalese people. The Gyalbo was seen to be the actual ruler of Lhasa, under the control of the Chinese *amban* or resident. Lhasa had its own standing army of about 1,000 Tibetan soldiers, armed with long flintlock guns.

The city was surrounded by mountains. The Dalai Lama lived in the Potala Palace, located at the foot of a low hill, a mile to the west (or about 2 km) of the city centre. The fort looked grand, with its walls, white in the blinding light, and gilded square towers. It was a mile and and a half in circumference (2.4 km) and about 300 feet above the surrounding ground. Steps led up to it from every side.

Notes on Lhasa

Nain Singh made detailed notes of the city and its people. The diet of the inhabitants consisted chiefly of salted butter-tea and meat of various kinds. Crops such as wheat and barley were cheap. The people wore ornaments of coral, pearls, precious stones, and occasionally of gold and silver. The few houses of the rich were built of brick and stone; most others lived in mud houses.

Lhasa received its supply of water from wells for the use of which a monthly tax of two annas was imposed on every house. In winter, merchants from China, the kingdoms of Central Asia –Tawang, Bhutan, Sikkim, Nepal, Darjeeling and Ladakh – brought their merchandise. There were even a few merchants from Azimabad, as present-day Patna in Bihar was called in these times. From China came tea, silks of all varieties, carpets and chinaware; from Central Asia, gold thread, silks, precious stones, horse saddles, sheep and valuable horses.

Musk – a fragrance obtained from the Himalayan deer found in these parts – eventually found its way to Europe via Nepal. Rice and other grain varieties that were foreign to Lhasa, were brought from Tawang in present-day Arunachal Pradesh and Bhutan. From Sikkim came rice and tobacco, and from Nepal, Darjeeling and Azimabad, broadcloth (obtained from wool), silks, satins, saddles, precious stones, coral, pearls, sugar, spices and a variety of other Indian commodities. The merchants returned to the plains in March before the rains made the rivers unfordable.

The strangest things found plentifully in Lhasa were fossils. Once crushed and powdered, these were said to possess healing properties when applied to wounds. One fossil particularly intrigued Nain Singh: it was a skull about two and a half feet long and equally broad.

Silver and Gold

Four miles or about seven kilometres to Lhasa's north was a long hill called 'Totiphu', which stretched east to west. This was reported to contain a great quantity of silver, yet the administration prohibited anyone from excavating or mining it, for the belief was that the country would be impoverished if the silver was mined indiscriminately. The same belief extended to gold, which was found in nearby areas, and yet extracted only in very small quantities. If the priests or anyone discovered a nugget of large size, it was immediately placed back in the earth, for such nuggets, the belief went, had life and grew in size over time.

Nain Singh wanted to follow the course of the river that flowed south of the city. The River Lhasa was believed to flow into the Yarlung Tsangpo (called the Brahmaputra in India), but he was informed that such a journey could be dangerous, unless he went with a well-armed party of at least a dozen men.

His stay in Lhasa ended up being long and Nain Singh was soon exhausted of funds. Once again, he supported himself by teaching accounting and book-keeping to Nepalese merchants.

AN OLD MAP OF LHASA

'Losar' Festivities

The New Year commenced with the new moon appearing around 15 February. The Tibetans called it the 'Losar'. On the eve of new year's day, the entire city was swept clean and the houses whitewashed. The following day, every house rooftop was decorated with festival flags, and there was much singing, dancing, and drinking of *chhang* or barley beer. Some of their special foods for this occasion included a kind of sweet rice called *droma dresil* and fried pastries known as *khapse*.

The Road to Gartok

Early in April 1866, Nain Singh learnt that his Ladakhi companions were about to head out for their return journey. They took the long road made largely of stone and soil that ran east to west, from Lhasa to Gartok, for a length of 800 miles (1200 km).

To help the traveller, every few miles, a triangle of stones was erected, each surmounted with a flag. The Tibetans viewed these stone piles as guideposts and objects of veneration. Travellers usually contributed a stone or two, or even a small folded piece of cloth as they went past, .

Between Lhasa and Gartok, there were 22 resting places or *tasams*, usually 20 to 70 miles apart (40 to 100 km), where the pack or draught animals were rested and changed. The *tasams* usually consisted of a house or houses made of dried bricks. The larger *tasams* had room for between 150 and 200 men at a time, and the smaller ones could house about a dozen people. Sometimes, people were accommodated in tents.

When he found himself on the road, between these resting places, Nain Singh slept in a rough tent where he and everyone out on the road experienced the fierce cold and biting wind. The yaks and donkeys carried a good supply of ordinary necessities such as grain, barley-meal, tea and butter. A necessary supply of fuel came from *argols* or dried dung from draught animals. Each camp was supposed to leave behind at least as much dried dung as it burnt as a gesture of courtesy to other travellers.

When walking along the great road, Nain Singh and his companions rose early. Before starting their march, they brewed themselves some tea. The Tibetans boiled their tea in water, adding in gram flour and butter; the tea leaves were always chewed. Another round of the brew was made at midday. At the end of every day, they had more tea to stave off hunger pangs till they had a meal ready of buckwheat cakes and meat. A caravan usually moved from dawn till 2 or 3 p.m., but sometimes they did not reach a camping ground till late in the evening.

Two months later, around early June 1866, Nain Singh reached the watershed area, i.e., the low area where the rivers Brahmaputra (Tsangpo) and Sutlej originated. Soon after, he arrived at Darchen, between the lakes Mansarovar and Raksastal. Here, before parting with his Ladakhi friends, he met a trader from Kumaon who knew him and helped him pay off the debts he had incurred during this long journey.

He finally crossed the Himalayan range on 26 June 1866 and arrived in British-held territory after being away for a year and more.

The Amazing Nain Singh

Nain Singh was able to make an elaborate route survey from Kathmandu to Tradom, and then again from Lhasa to Gartok. Later on, during other expeditions, he helped define most of the Tsangpo's course from its source near Lake Mansarovar to the point where it joined the River Lhasa, its tributary. In another exploration – Nain Singh made three in all – he made a careful route survey from Lukung, west of Pangong Lake in Ladakh, to Lhasa and from here to Odalguri, Assam.

During his last journey, almost a decade after his first, Nain Singh suffered periods of poor health. His eyesight was seriously affected from constant exposure to the cold, wind and the blinding glare of the mountain sun. The long journeys proved testing in various ways. After he returned from his last expedition in 1873, Nain Singh retired with a well-earned pension. In the early 1890s, he went to Moradabad, Uttar Pradesh, to look after his estate granted as a reward by the British Government and died there in 1895 after an illness.

Nain Singh's explorations set the base for later surveyors and explorers to Tibet and the Himalayan region. He won universal admiration for his persistence and observational skills, especially his unique ability to blend in and cleverly find his way out of a difficult situation. His reports, later documented and translated by his superior, Thomas Montgomerie, who then headed these survey missions, proved immensely valuable. Today, a journey from Kathmandu to Lhasa – about 800 miles (1,100 km) apart – is possible by aeroplane and even by road, and it reminds us of Nain Singh's admirable and courageous endeavours.

7

A HEADMASTER'S SECRET JOURNEYS

SARAT CHANDRA DAS BEFRIENDS A LAMA

The mysteriousness of Lhasa, a city 'forbidden' to foreigners, enthralled this scholar, who made two journeys to it at great cost not just to his own life but also to the lives of those who helped him.

In the beginning, from the mid-nineteenth century onwards, the British administration in India explored Tibet in total secret. The British hoped not just to understand the terrain, but other things about this mysterious land: What kind of society people lived in, how their communities functioned, their language and their ways of living, and especially, how the rulers thought. The last bit mattered to the British as they strengthened their hold on South Asia and sought to keep rivals at bay. China, though defeated, was a big kingdom, and so was Russia to the north-west of Afghanistan. It was thus important for the British that kingdoms and their rulers on India's frontier like Nepal, Tibet and even Afghanistan were allied to British Indian interests.

In the eastern Himalayas, where passes to Tibet lay across the Kanchenjunga, the initial surveys were carried out by three 'pundits'. They were associated with a school called the Bhotia (also spelled Bhutia) Boarding School set up in Darjeeling in April 1874.

This school aimed to educate boys from the nearby Tibetan and Sikkimese communities. More critically, as British officials openly admitted, it existed to create a band of trained interpreters, geographers and explorers who could prove to be useful in the future if and when Tibet decided to allow outsiders, including the British, into its territory. The syllabus covered both traditional Tibetan language and religion, as well as subjects like mathematics and English. Sarat Chandra Das was its first headmaster.

Dreams of Travel

Sarat Chandra was born in Chittagong in East Bengal (present-day Bangladesh) and studied civil engineering in Calcutta (now Kolkata). He was recommended for the position of headmaster of the Bhotia Boarding School in Darjeeling when he was only twenty-five.

In 1876, Das happened to read a book edited by Clements R. Markham, titled *Narratives of the Mission of George Manning to Tibet and Journey of Thomas Manning to Lhasa*. Das was greatly impressed and inspired. Right away, he wanted to visit Lhasa to be an explorer just like the people he had read about.

He spoke about his wish to his friend Lama Ugyen Gyatso, who taught Tibetan at the same school.

However, securing permission to enter Tibet from British officials proved difficult. Sarat Chandra then had a brainwave: he would get his friend, Lama Ugyen, to make a visit to Tibet, especially to the great monastery of Tashi Lhunpo near Shigatze, which was the seat of the Panchen Lama. Ugyen Gyatso, who came from an illustrious family, would travel as a representative of his own monastery at Pemionchi, carrying appropriate tribute.

SARAT CHANDRA DAS

While in Tibet, Lama Ugyen would speak to influential lamas and secure for Das an invitation and passport to enter Tibet. The lama agreed to the mission, provided he was given leave from teaching at the school and funds to cover his expenses.

Beyond the Kanchenjunga

Things worked out just as Das had hoped. In September 1878, Lama Ugyen returned, and he had the prized document, a passport, issued by the Panchen Lama. Sengchen Kyabying, chief minister to the Panchen Lama at Tashi Lhunpo, had been most helpful.

The chief minister was interested in learning the languages the Buddha had preached in and know more about the land where his teachings were popular. Lama Ugyen, sensing an opportunity, suggested Das as the right teacher, and the passport was granted almost at once, with the permission of the Panchen Lama. The passport provided for assistance with ponies and other draught animals, food and accommodation for the journey of Sarat Chandra and Lama Ugyen into and out of Tibet.

Sarat Chandra convinced his wife of his journey by telling her that Shigatze and Tibet were only a few miles from Darjeeling and he was not likely to be away for too long!

Sarat Chandra first proceeded to Calcutta with Lama Ugyen. There, under the watch of British officials, Sarat Chandra's rusty knowledge of surveying, dating from his days as an engineering student, was brought up to speed for the purpose of secret exploration by Nain Singh. The latter instructed both Sarat Chandra and the lama in using the sextant, the compass, and the method of figuring out the altitude using the thermometer and boiling water. It was quite a simple method, but Sarat Chandra had to remember it! The boiling point of water is 100°C at sea level, and the temperature decreases by about 0.5°C with a rise of every 540 feet.

Returning to Darjeeling, Sarat Chandra Das and Lama Ugyen, together with a guide and two coolies, set out in June 1879. In addition to surveying equipment, they had two guns hidden away, along with a pair of binoculars, a camera, a photography manual and 150 rupees in cash.

Travelling north into Sikkim, they reached Jongri on 17 June and then turned north-west towards the Nepal border. Wherever they halted every night, Das boiled water and measured its temperature to determine their altitude. He also tried, weather permitting, to take sextant observations of the stars. Lama Ugyen assisted him and took other necessary measurements during their march.

Ordeals of Passage

Once they had crossed the frontier into Nepal, they spent several days at the Gyunsar Monastery, which was affiliated to Lama Ugyen's home monastery at Pemionchi. The monks mistook Sarat Chandra for a fellow lama. The Gyunsar lamas were very helpful. They provided new coolies and a guide named Phurchung to assist them on their onward journey. The travellers left hurriedly on receiving news that the passes were about to be closed to prevent the spread of a cattle disease into Tibet.

The journey had not been an easy one so far. Mist and rain hampered the route survey work in Sikkim, and Sarat Chandra suffered from altitude sickness across the pass into Nepal. The scenery, though, was magnificent. Lofty mountains of red rock towered over small villages set amid wooded valleys. As they proceeded, immense rock walls, marking the base of Mount Kanchenjunga, were visible to the east. By the time they reached the pass into Tibet, Sarat Chandra was noticeably exhausted and the guide, Phurchung, had to carry him on his back over the uneven terrain and snowy patches.

The Lama Friend

They reached Shigatze on 7 July and Sarat Chandra, in the book he wrote later, described the Tashi Lhunpo

Monastery as 'a dazzling hill of polished gold'. The Panchen Lama was away, and the chief minister, Sengchen Kyabying (or Sengchen Lama), who had assured a passport for Sarat Chandra, received them warmly. He repeated his desire to study Hindustani and Sanskrit, and to learn how to operate a camera and develop photographs and how to use telescope as well, which he had recently bought from a Kashmiri merchant.

Das and Lama Ugyen remained at Tashi Lhunpo for two and a half months. Eager for information, the chief minister delighted in the books and the 'magic lantern' (which projected images on a screen or wall) they had brought to Tashi Lhunpo. The minister shut himself off from the outside world for two weeks, so the visitors could spend all their time with him. He refused admission to other visitors and pilgrims.

The Panchen Lama's Suspicions

When the Panchen Lama returned to Tashi Lhunpo in August, Sarat Chandra was granted an audience. He described the Panchen as being 'twenty-six years of age, of a spare frame and middling stature. He has a remarkably broad forehead and large eyes, slightly oblique'. The young boy Nain Singh had described meeting in 1865 was now considerably grown up!

No words were exchanged at the audience, but Sarat Chandra was informed that his request to stay on as a theology student at Tashi Lhunpo had been granted. The Panchen Lama, however, suspected that both Sarat Chandra and Lama Ugyen were British agents, and ordered monks to camp in shifts at Sarat Chandra's quarters under the pretext of studying Tibetan scriptures. Sarat Chandra was no fool and he posed tough and profound questions on Buddhism to them. The students were usually at a loss and couldn't supply the right answers. Soon, their numbers dwindled and then died away altogether.

Later that month, Sarat Chandra left for Darjeeling with Lama Ugyen. The Panchen Lama granted them a passport that required the headman of every village on the way to help them with food and shelter. He also made available 10 yaks and three ponies for their journey. They left with 40 Tibetan manuscripts.

The chief minister, or Sengchen Byakying, urged Sarat Chandra to bring back with him a lithographic press (the chief minister made an initial down payment), smallpox vaccines, a music box and other goods in a long list of items. As an incentive, the chief minister promised to take Sarat Chandra with him to Lhasa the following year. On 10 November 1879, after an absence of five months, the two men returned to Darjeeling.

The route survey to Shigatze produced from the observations made by Sarat Chandra and Lama Ugyen proved very useful. Equally crucial were their notes on Tibetan customs, religion and language. But more vitally, an informal diplomatic link had been established with a sympathetic official in Tibet, and as the British officials agreed, a second visit would make the connection an enduring one.

Another Journey

Local disturbances in Sikkim made a return visit to Tibet in 1880 impossible. That year, Sarat Chandra spent his time writing at his home in Darjeeling (aptly called 'Lhasa Villa') and improving his knowledge of Tibetan history, religion and language. He also worked on his surveying skills.

By 1881, conditions in Sikkim had improved somewhat and, in July, Sarat Chandra sought permission from the authorities again. He wished to explore the territory between Lhasa and Peking (now Beijing). The government, however, was prepared to sanction an expedition only as far as Lhasa, with a stop at the Tashi Lhunpo Monastery at Shigatze.

On 7 November 1881, Sarat Chandra and Lama Ugyen again accompanied by their guide Phurchung, left for Tibet. They carried with them 5,000-rupees worth of gold, coral, pearls and other saleable commodities to cover their expenses en route. This was a big improvement over the allowances they had received for their first journey, when Sarat Chandra had had to finance himself for the most part.

Once beyond the environs of Darjeeling, Sarat Chandra disguised himself as a Tibetan lama. There had been disturbances earlier, and outsiders, especially from India, were viewed with greater suspicion and resentment. They took the same route as earlier, and Das arrived at Tashi Lhunpo on 9 December.

The chief minister was away but had left instructions for the visitors to be treated well. Sarat Chandra renewed old acquaintances and learnt more about the religious practices at Tashi Lhunpo. He resumed his studies of Tibetan and Sanskrit books. As they waited for the chief minister's return, Das heard that most of their heavy luggage, dispatched separately from Darjeeling, had been held up on the frontier on the orders of a Tibetan official at a border outpost called Khamba Jong. This luggage contained, among other things, the smallpox vaccine and the lithographic press the chief minister had so desired. Sarat Chandra sent the faithful Phurchung to secure his luggage, but the latter had little luck.

A Reunion with a Friend

Meanwhile, Sarat Chandra received a request from the Sengchen Lama to meet him at Dongtse, 35 miles (56 km) south-east of Tashi Lhunpo and on the road to Gyantse. This was the chief minister's native village. Sarat Chandra and Lama Ugyen were gladly welcomed when they reached, and the three men picked up their discussions from where they had left off in 1879.

The chief minister showed Sarat Chandra a manuscript that he was working on. It had a section on photography, complete with diagrams borrowed from the photography manual Sarat Chandra had brought him on his first journey. This time, the chief minister hoped to study English with Sarat Chandra.

On their return to Tashi Lhunpo, the chief minister, always keen to learn new things, asked to be shown how the prismatic compass operated. He requested a few surveying instruments, plus a medicine chest and a book on astronomy. Lama Ugyen replied that this needed a trip back to Calcutta, and that Sarat Chandra would be left alone if he left, but the chief minister, helpful as always, came up with his own plan. He suggested that Sarat Chandra could go to Lhasa with the Panchen Lama, who had to travel there for the ordination ceremony of the new Dalai Lama.

When the lithographic press finally arrived from the border post, the chief minister and Sarat Chandra assembled it with great joy. They were like two boys with building blocks! The rest of the luggage, however, remained stuck at the frontier. The chief minister was now even more insistent about Lama Ugyen returning to the border. He provided the latter with a suitable passport as well.

On 28 January Lama Ugyen left Tashi Lhunpo, accompanied by Phurchung. Sarat Chandra stayed back and continued his studies, trying to teach the chief minister the rudiments of telegraphy, as well as English and arithmetic. All the while, he looked forward avidly to his promised visit to Lhasa.

He left on his own for Lhasa on 20 April 1882.

Troubles on the Road

There were reports of an outbreak of smallpox in Lhasa, yet Sarat Chandra decided to press on. He first headed for Dongtse and then passed through Gyantse. Then, he turned eastward and followed the route taken by Nain Singh in 1865. He soon arrived, like Nain Singh, on the west bank of the Yamdrok Lake. He described it as shaped irregularly like a scorpion, with a large, curved piece of land stretching into the water. However, Das soon fell sick with a high fever.

Luckily, a caravan accompanying the wife of a high-ranking Lhasa official soon camped in the area. The lady's cousin was the abbess of the nearby monastery of Samding. The caravan departed without Sarat Chandra, who was considerably weak after his sudden fever. The official's wife, though afraid that he had somehow contracted smallpox, left him with necessary supplies of food, as well as a letter of introduction to the abbess.

Thanks to her help, Sarat Chandra received good care at Samding. He remained there, weak from fever, for the next ten days. Eventually he recovered after taking in medication that included, as he wrote later, 'a sacred pill' said to contain a particle of the holy Buddha's relics. In gratitude, and as per custom, Das arranged for the purchase of 500 freshly caught fish, which were promptly returned to the lake. This act earned him great merit according to traditional Buddhist beliefs.

Following the lake on foot as he went onward, Sarat Chandra reached the River Tsangpo and saw the iron-chain bridge across it that Nain Singh had written about after his second journey to Lhasa in 1866. The melting snow was high enough to reach the bridge, and so Sarat Chandra, taking no risk, crossed over by boat. Finally, he reached Lhasa, the city of his dreams, on 30 May 1882.

Lhasa Days

Jostling with merchants and travellers keen to enter the city, Das entered unquestioned. His fatigued appearance and dark eyeglasses made people believe he was a sick man. He found accommodation in a building where lamas from Tashi Lhunpo usually lodged, and he soon set about exploring the city, mapping its streets and temples, buying Tibetan books and witnessing a religious ritual at the main temple of Lhasa.

He managed a brief and formal audience with the Dalai Lama. Sarat Chandra described him as a 'child of eight with a bright and fair complexion and rosy cheeks'. Thupten Gyatso, the thirteenth Dalai Lama, with whom Das had an audience, lived until 1933. As smallpox spread in Lhasa, Sarat Chandra was forced to cut his stay short and return to Tashi Lhunpo. On the way back, he stopped again at Dongtse to meet his friend, the chief minister. The latter too had contracted smallpox, though he would recover soon. Das pressed on toward Shigatze and met up with Phurchung and Lama Ugyen, who gave him letters from India.

At this point, rumours began circulating that Sarat Chandra was a British agent. His presence had been noticed in Lhasa and reported to concerned officials. Das realized he had to leave for India to stave off danger. Lama Ugyen went on ahead with the botanical and other scientific data he had collected, and Das left Tashi Lhunpo with Phurchung on 18 October. He was determined to visit the famous monastery of Samye, the first monastery built in Tibet, around 775 CE, on the banks of the Tsangpo.

Sarat Chandra spent several days exploring the monastery and the surrounding countryside. On one of these excursions, he followed the Tsangpo as far

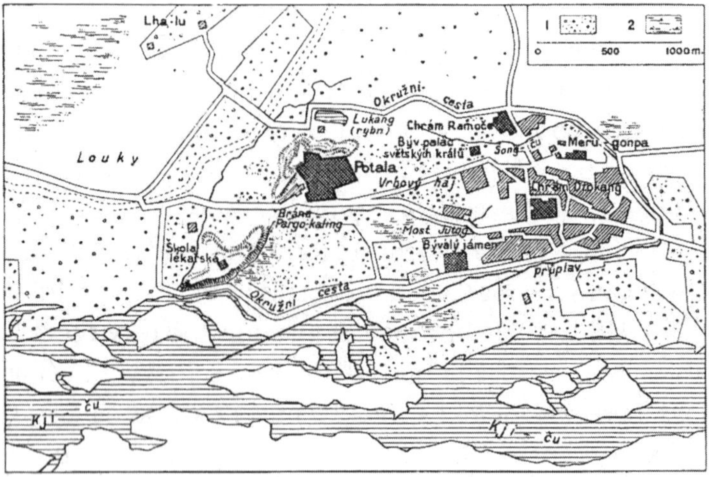

Obr. 204. *Plán Lhasy, podle Rydera a Waddella.*

1. Zahrady. — 2. Močály. — Měřítko 1:38.500.

OLD LHASA MAP

downriver as Chetang (Tsetang). Here, a Kashmiri merchant voiced suspicions about Sarat Chandra's true identity, and the latter left hurriedly again and returned to Tashi Lhunpo by a different route. His friend, the chief minister, came to his aid again and issued a passport giving Sarat Chandra permission to proceed to India and to return to Tibet in the near future. The Panchen Lama had died in the meantime.

Northwards Again

Sarat Chandra left for Darjeeling but made a brief halt at yet another monastery, the Sakya Monastery founded in 1073 CE. Then he moved south toward Khamba Jong, the border post between Sikkim and Tibet. He finally reached Darjeeling on 27 December.

In addition to the geographical and other data that Das returned with, he also had with him over 200 volumes of works, manuscripts and block-prints, many in Sanskrit, which had not been seen in India for centuries. These texts had been transported by earlier monks almost a thousand or so years ago. All this material helped Das produce a good deal of scholarly material over time, including collaborating on a voluminous Tibetan-English dictionary that was published in Calcutta in 1902.

In October 1884, Sarat Chandra accompanied a British civil officer, Colman Macaulay, to Tibet. They reached Peking (now Beijing) a year later in 1885. Das was in his usual monk's disguise. His learning and tact soon made him quite popular, and he was sought after by the lamas in Peking. He took up residence in a monastery where mainly monks of the 'Yellow Hat' sect gathered. (The name Yellow Hat comes from the yellow headdress worn by the Dge-lugs-pa monks to differentiate them from the Karma-pa sect, whose monks wear red headgear.)

While he was there, he gained a lot of useful intelligence information. To pass this on to his superiors, he had to be discreet and think on his feet. He wore his yellow monk's robes in a covered carriage to a friend's house, where he changed into Indian clothes, and then proceeded in another enclosed vehicle to where the British officers had put up.

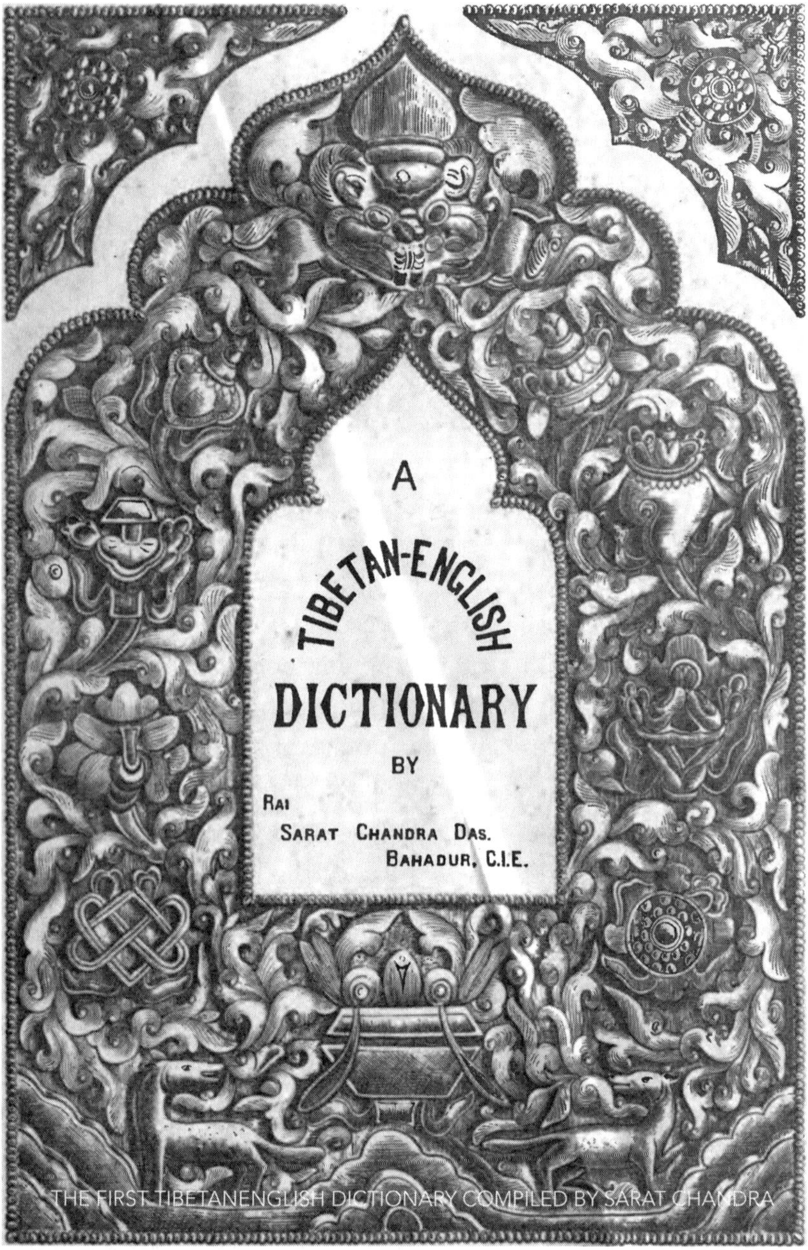

THE FIRST TIBETANENGLISH DICTIONARY COMPILED BY SARAT CHANDRA

Other Travellers to Tibet

Sarat Chandra had made it to Tibet thrice, but other foreigners did not quite have the same luck. During Sarat Chandra's time in Tibet in 1879, the Russian geographer Nikolai Przhevalsky tried to enter the country but was pointedly turned back. The important Tibetan monasteries, alarmed by reports of his travel, gathered 3,000 monks between them to halt his progress. Przhevalsky died on his next attempt to reach Lhasa a few years later.

Earlier that same year, a Hungarian expedition under Count Bela Szechenyi had set rumours ablaze in Lhasa, as he tried to enter Tibet from western China. Like Przhevalsky, he was forced to give up.

Thomas Manning, an Englishman, had gained an entry in 1811, as had the French Christian priests, Evariste Regis Hue and Joseph Gabet, who visited in 1846. But things became difficult in the late 1880s, for Tibet clearly wished to remain isolated.

Losing a Friend

The later discovery of the real nature of Sarat Chandra's mission by the Tibetan authorities only increased their desire to debar travellers from entering Tibet.

Additionally, those who had helped Sarat Chandra and Lama Ugyen paid a heavy price for their actions.

In 1887, Sengchen Kyabying, the Panchen Lama's chief minister, accused of helping foreigners, was subjected to daily public beatings in the Lhasa marketplace. He finally succumbed to his injuries and his body was thrown into the river. The governor of Gyantse and his wife, who had helped Sarat Chandra on the instructions of the chief minister, were imprisoned for life, their helpers mutilated and left to die.

The Japanese monk and scholar Ekai Kawaguchi, who had studied under Sarat Chandra during 1898–99 in Darjeeling before proceeding to Lhasa, was also later questioned by Tibetan officials about Sarat Chandra.

As for Sarat Chandra, he returned to Darjeeling and settled down to a life of scholarship. He continued to work for the Bengal government as a Tibetan translator. In 1886, he was awarded the Marquess of Dufferin and Ava's Silver Medal by the British Indian government for his services. The following year he was honoured by the king of Siam (now Thailand) as well for his understanding of Buddhist theology. In 1892, he founded the Buddhist Text Society of India and became its first secretary. The British Indian government also bestowed on him the title of Rai Bahadur and made him a 'Companion of the Order of the Indian Empire'.

When the British finally succeeded in formally opening a relationship with Tibet in 1904 with the Francis Younghusband Expedition that year, they were indebted for many details on their maps, and for the description of Lhasa, to Sarat Chandra Das, Lama Ugyen and the Indian explorers who had gone there before, like Nain Singh.

Around 1914 or 1915, Sarat Chandra moved to Calcutta. There, in 1915, he renewed his friendship with Ekai Kawaguchi, who persuaded him to travel to Japan with him. Sarat Chandra did travel to Japan in 1916, though he had only just recovered from a long illness. He died a few months later, probably in Japan, on 5 January 1917.

Sarat Chandra Das found a place in fiction too. In 1901, when Rudyard Kipling wrote his famous novel, *Kim*, the character of the secret agent Huree Chunder Mookerjee was believed to be based on Sarat Chandra.

8

THE MYSTERIES OF A RIVER

KINTHUP FOLLOWS THE BRAHMAPUTRA

A tailor by profession and a guide by passion made the journey upriver to find the exact origin of the River Brahmaputra, and found himself spending years in captivity.

In the 1850s, as the British in India expanded their reach across Assam and the provinces beyond, they grew ever more curious about the River Brahmaputra. They wanted to know where it flowed from, its origin from beyond the Himalayas, and if it was the same as the River Tsangpo. All they had was knowledge from traders and wanderers. The Tsangpo, these travellers said, flowed from beyond the northern slopes of the Himalayas for 1,300 km before turning south-west and flowing down into the Assam valley. The river, it was noted, dropped by as much as 11,000 metres within a mere distance of 300 km. Travelling missionaries believed that this became the River Irrawaddy that flowed into Burma (Myanmar). This assumption later turned out to be a mistake, but the British still needed confirmation about this majestic river.

The Brahmaputra's Mysteries

East to where the River Tsangpo enters the Himalayas north of the Indian subcontinent, there are four other rivers separated by only 80 km or so from each other: The Irrawaddy that flows toward Myanmar, the Yangtze that flows through China, and the rivers Mekong and Salween later flowing through South-East Asia.

The expedition to track the Brahmaputra to its origins began upriver from Assam. The exercise was complicated because four rivers joined to form the Brahmaputra as it flowed into Assam through the Himalayas. The easternmost of these is the River Lohit, in present-day east Arunachal Pradesh, and the rivers flowing west to this are the rivers Dibang, Dihang (or Siang) and Subansiri.

Nain Singh, as we know, followed the river Tsangpo (Brahmaputra) from Mansarovar eastward to its tributary that flowed by Lhasa. In 1874, he reached Chetang (now called Tsetang), south-east of Lhasa, to follow the Brahmaputra as it flowed downstream, but he had to return as he was running out of funds.

Harman and His Theories

After a British surveyor, Lieutenant Henry Harman, measured the flow of these four rivers as they moved through Assam, he realized it was the Dihang/Siang, which had the highest volume of water among all four rivers. It was this river that needed to be traced right back to the higher Himalayas and beyond. It had the largest volume of water, which meant, Harman surmised, that it received waters from smaller streams and so there was every chance that this was the river called Tsangpo, which became the Brahmaputra later as it entered Upper Assam (now Arunachal Pradesh).

In 1878, he sought out two men from Sikkim: Nem Singh, and his associate, Kinthup. Nem Singh was Harman's Tibetan teacher in Darjeeling. He was a lama from the celebrated Pemionchi Monastery. Nem Singh was about 30 years old, and a Bhutia from Sikkim. Besides Tibetan and other local languages, he knew a bit of English. He worked for the Public Works Department, overseeing labourers employed on contract, and was also an occasional interpreter at the Court of Darjeeling.

A Scared Traveller

Nem Singh and Kinthup, who travelled as the former's helper, left Darjeeling for the Chumbi Valley, an area in south Tibet that extended towards Sikkim and Bhutan. They passed through Phari (now called Pagri, near the Bhutan–Tibet border). They were soon at Lake Yamdrok, approaching it from the west.

Nem Singh, also code-named G.M.N. by his British superiors including Harman, provided a good description of the great chain bridge that Nain Singh Rawat, an explorer employed by the British, had mentioned in one of his earlier expeditions to this region, and that Sarat Chandra Das, a scholar who too had journeyed to Tibet, had seen as well. It was, to Nem Singh, the most wonderful thing he had ever seen. It was made of four iron chains about 300 paces long (a pace is a normal human step, about 30 or so inches). A rope footway was suspended from two chains on either side. The chains themselves were meshed around huge wooden pillars sunk into the river. The bridge allowed for safe passage, one person at a time, but shook violently in the wind. When it rained, boats were used to cross the lake.

Nem Singh and Kinthup finally reached Lhasa and presented gifts (presumably out of survey funds) to the lamas as an act of devotion. On leaving the city, they made their way to Chetang (Tsetang), and in October 1878, they began the journey downriver.

A few miles out of Chetang, the road no longer followed the Tsangpo and instead went north. Eventually, it did bend back to rejoin the river. Where the road left the river, the latter turned in a south-easterly direction. Nem Singh noted, though, that this south-easterly flow continued for only a very short distance before the river turned east and then made a sharp turn north-east. This was a new and major discovery.

The river flowed right through the two main peaks of the eastern Himalayas – Namcha Barwa and Gyala Peri (both above 23,000 feet). Nem Singh and Kinthup crossed Pei, the place where the river entered the mountains, and reached the outpost, then known as Gyala Sindong. It was here that Nem Singh felt intimidated by the sheer height of the mountains around him, the dense forests and the ferocity of the rapids. The canyon the river flows through is the deepest around Pei, and at 504 km, it is longer than even the Grand Canyon (446 km long) in America. The river at this point presents a majestic, breathtaking sight, as it loses height by a series of falls, descending from 9,500 to 4,900 feet, and then another 2,200 feet as it enters India.

A Displeased Boss

Though Nem Singh, along with Kinthup, was the first explorer to get beyond Chetang, Harman was not happy. Nem Singh was unable to provide much information of his return route and failed at times to make proper entries in his field book. While travelling along the great bend of the Tsangpo, Nem Singh had been in great fear of robbers and was in a big hurry to leave the area, and his recordings proved to be very inaccurate. He was sent to Nain Singh for further training in survey work.

Four years later, following his own survey work of the mountains near north Sikkim, Harman remembered Kinthup, who had made quite an impression on him. Kinthup, then 31 years old, was described by Harman in his correspondence with the Royal Geographical Society in London as 'dependable, thickset, of medium height and with a look of dogged determination. He had weather-beaten features and a deep voice' along with the 'alertness of a mountaineer and the strength of a lion'.

Kinthup on a Mission

Kinthup had also shown himself to be a reliable companion and helper. He was already familiar with the Tsangpo's route from Lhasa to Chetang, and as far as Gyala Sindong. Kinthup could easily have been an explorer in his own right, but he had neither been schooled nor trained to record field observations methodically. As things turned out, it was Kinthup's phenomenal memory and his accurate description of places that helped early surveyors pin down quite a bit of the Brahmaputra mystery.

Harman teamed him up with a Chinese lama – whose name, for some reason, was never recorded – for whom he was to act as assistant. Kinthup had already worked as a guide for travellers to upper Sikkim. For his daily bread, though, he ran a tailoring shop in Darjeeling.

In 1880, disguised as pilgrims, Kinthup and the lama headed north from Sikkim towards Gyala Sindong. Their instructions were to move beyond this outpost, tracing the Tsangpo's flow. To make sure things went right, Harman devised an ingenious plan. The two were to prepare a large number of logs, and place into niches carved into these logs, the especially marked 'tubes' they were carrying. After sending a message to Harman, the logs were to be thrown into the Tsangpo. Floating down the river, once these logs were found by Harman's men stationed at the point where the Dihang entered Assam, it would establish once and for all the proposition that the Dihang did indeed join the Tsangpo to the Brahmaputra.

KINTHUP

In a Lama's Company

The two crossed the Donkia Pass (or Dongkha La) on 7 August 1880, the same pass Hooker had passed, as had Sarat Chandra Das and Lama Ugyen some time ago. They halted for two days at the Cholamo Lake as they waited for transport to Gyantse. Whenever questioned about their destination, Kinthup had a standard reply: the lama with whom he was travelling was going to pay a visit to his sister, and he was accompanying him as a helper.

Once across the border into Tibet, they joined a group of merchants for the seven-day journey to Gyantse. They remained for nearly a week here, while the lama was entertained by old friends visiting from the Sera Monastery, one of the three great monasteries, together with Drepung and Ganden, on the outskirts of Lhasa (as Nain Singh too had noted).

They continued to travel by begging for food and halting at *jikkiyop*s (or resting places) erected by the Tibetan government to protect travellers from inclement weather and wild animals. Sometimes they spent the nights in caves. By end-August they reached Chetang. The lama fell sick here. For his part, Kinthup, as he later recounted, had already begun to feel 'badly treated' and bullied by his companion.

Once the lama recovered, they continued, always keeping the river in sight. An unexpected delay occurred in the village of Thun Tsung, where they had intended to stay for only two days. The lama, it seemed, did not have the heart to leave. A hapless Kinthup was forced to remain there for four months before they could finally leave. In this way, in fits and starts, they reached Gyala Sindong in March 1881.

They never left the river all through this, and walking along its banks, soon came to the village of Pemakochung, which had a small monastery. Only two miles (3.5 km) away, as Kinthup later reported, the Tsangpo 'fell over a cliff, from a height of about 150 feet'. Kinthup recollected how the falling water, in play with the light, shaped rainbows at the foot of the mountain.

Sold into Slavery

Kinthup and the lama then moved upriver and turned inland to Jongjuk Jong (now called Tongjuk/Tongkyuk), where the Tsangpo has its most northerly point. The bridge leading to Tongjuk was manned by an elderly man who checked for permits issued by the Dzongpen, the head of the district. There was a delay again as the lama and the elderly man left to get the necessary permit from the Dzongpen. Kinthup remained by the outpost fort near the bridge and looked for a chance to hide his three compasses and pistol. The lama returned four days later with the required permit. In the fort, Kinthup boarded with the Dzongpen's helpers, and they re-equipped themselves with flour, meat and tea needed for the next stage of the journey.

For Kinthup, though, things soon took a turn for the worse. The lama spent far too much time with the Dzongpen, and he worried the lama would soon disclose the real nature of their travel to him. Soon enough, one of the Dzongpen's helpers came up and threatened Kinthup with dire consequences if he didn't come clean about what he was hiding away. Kinthup was forced to disclose what he had stowed away – the compasses and his pistol.

Then, sometime in May 1881, the lama informed Kinthup quite nonchalantly that he was leaving on business but would return in two or three days. That was the last that Kinthup or anyone ever heard of him. Kinthup remained in the Dzongpen's fort for two months, where he soon learned that the lama had in fact sold him as a slave! Kinthup was engaged in menial work, and his skills as a tailor were also employed, yet he never lost patience and constantly looked for an opportunity to escape. He had managed to keep one of his compasses out of sight of the Dzongpen's men.

Making a Getaway

Almost a year later, as he recorded, on the evening of 7 March 1882, Kinthup managed to give everyone the slip. He fled first to a village on the Tsangpo, and then walked a further 20 miles (34 km) before he found himself in more mountainous terrain. He pressed on downriver to Marpung. He was barely 35 miles (56 km) from the outpost of Gyala Sindong when his pursuers caught up with him.

There was a small monastery in Marpung. Now terribly exhausted and running out of ideas, Kinthup sought help from the monastery's chief lama. He said he was a pilgrim and begged the lama not to hand him over to the Dzongpen's men. The lama intervened, but Kinthup had merely exchanged one form of slavery for another. Now he became lama's slave, who had just bought him out. After four and a half months, he asked the lama for a month's leave so he could make a pilgrimage. The lama, moved by his piety, readily gave permission.

It was, by now, August 1882. Kinthup had been away for two years and had twice been sold into slavery. But he remembered his instructions and wanted to carry out Harman's plan to the letter. Harman had suggested throwing marked logs into the River Tsangpo. But first these logs had to be gathered, and then a message had to reach Harman, whose men would check for these logs in the Dihang as it flowed through India.

A Lenient Lama

Kinthup utilized his 'leave' well. He gathered some five hundred logs (the number is perhaps not accurate). He was doubly careful about not being seen or even followed. Apparently, as records state, Kinthup stayed in a deserted cave for five days making special markings on the logs, all of which were around one foot long.

Kinthup had with him a few hundred tin tubes (again the numbers may not be accurate), each containing an identification paper. It is amazing how Kinthup had managed to keep these hidden away. He had also travelled with a gouge to drill holes in the logs; then the tubes were to be inserted into the logs. Kinthup had lost the gouge but retained the tubes. And he was nothing if not innovative. He tied a tube with bamboo

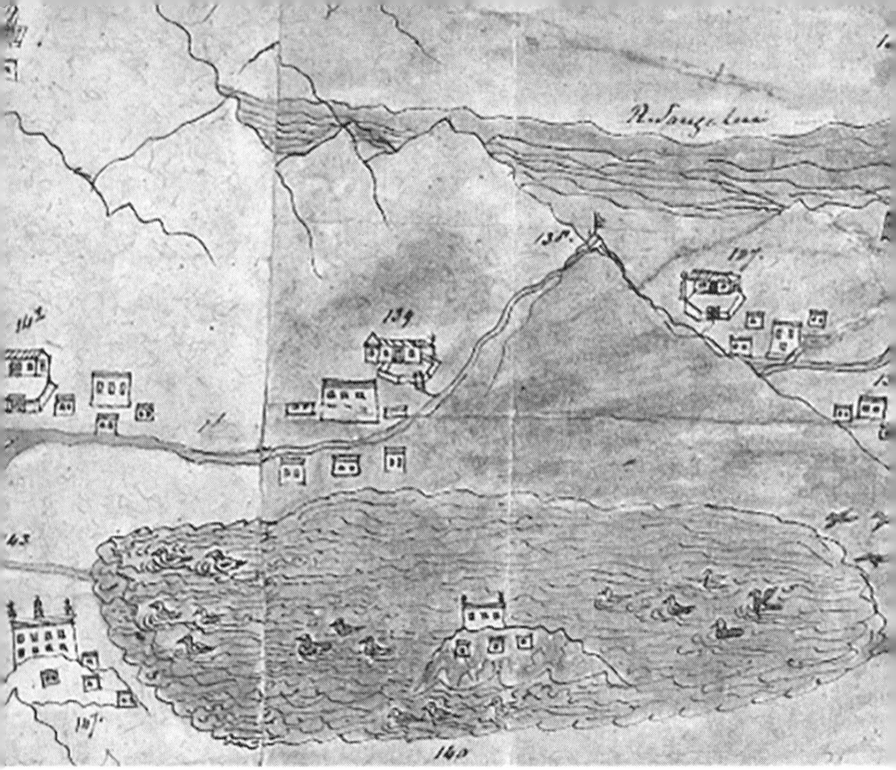

PICTURE-MAP OF CENTRAL TIBET, SHOWING YAMDROKTSO LAKE AND THE RIVER YARLUNG–TSANGPO

strips outside each log and kept them all safely hidden. It was all too much to do in five days, and later scholars now believe that he had spent about a month away from Marpung.

A Letter Back Home

Kinthup then returned to the lama, and after working for two months, he asked for leave again, this time intending to head for Lhasa. In December 1882, he reached Lhasa and penned a letter to Nem Singh. He hoped the letter would somehow reach Harman via

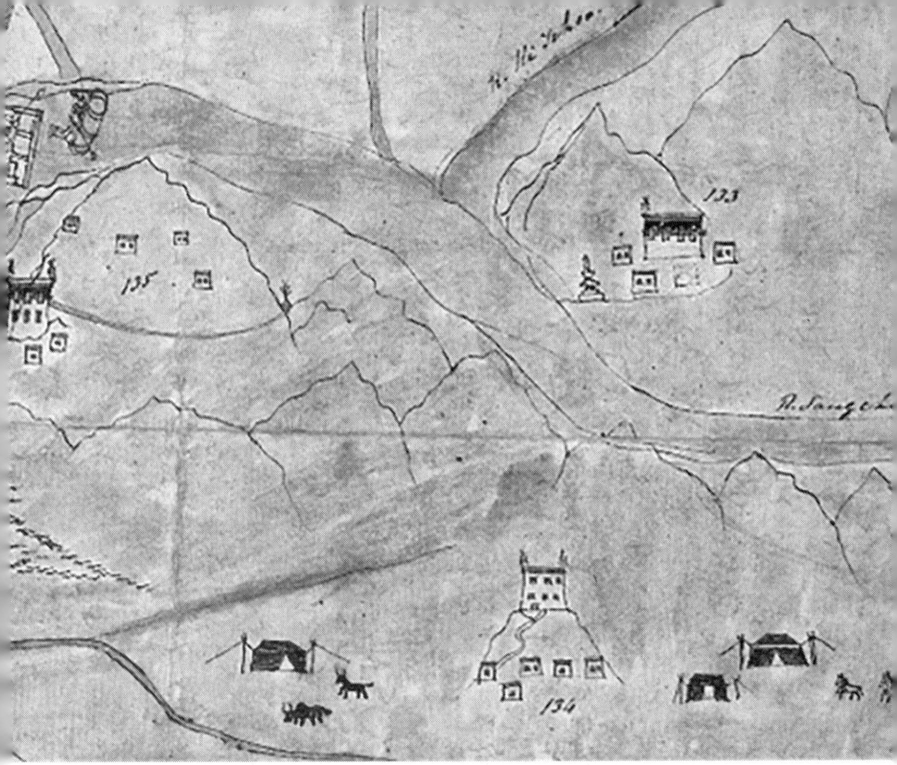

Nem Singh. Kinthup wrote about the logs and his idea of throwing around fifty logs a day into the Tsangpo. Kinthup even specified the time he would do so, according to the Tibetan calendar, which Nem Singh was familiar with.

This letter was written up for Kinthup by a *kazi* (judge) of Sikkim, whose wife took the letter to Darjeeling. Kinthup then returned to Marpung, and he finally secured his 'freedom' after another nine months.

The letter reached Nem Singh but was never delivered to Harman. By this time, the date for throwing the logs into the Tsangpo had already passed and Nem Singh did not take the letter seriously enough. Moreover, Harman had left India in December 1882, even before the letter reached. He still believed, having heard nothing of Kinthup or the lama, that they had been arrested or some worse ill-fortune had befallen them.

Harman was also affected by a bad case of frostbite. His expedition to the Kanchenjunga in 1881 had to be aborted and he had spent a year in Darjeeling, hoping to recuperate. When his condition deteriorated, he resigned from the Survey of India and left for Europe. He was cared for in his final months by his sisters, and he died in Florence, Italy, on 14 April 1883, after falling ill with pneumonia.

A Long Way Home

Kinthup stayed on in Tibet for a month longer. He was engaged by a man for a month in stitching clothes, in return for salt and food. When he was finally able to leave, he headed for the cave where he had hidden his special logs. He retrieved them, and then threw them into the river, at a rate of 50 per day. His intention was to try to follow the Tsangpo into India. He pressed on, but the road deteriorated even more southward, becoming only a track, impassable even on ponies.

He soon found himself in an area dominated by the hostile Abors (the word meant independent, and they are also known as the 'Adi' ethnic group). They were always suspicious of strangers, and armed themselves with the sword or bow and arrows to keep interlopers away.

At this time, he was only a little over 40 miles (64 km) from the boundary of British India. He was, however, forced to turn back, because the Adi people did not allow him to pass through their land. He retraced his steps along the Tsangpo and reached the monastery of Namchi in Sikkim. Here he encountered Nem Singh again, who at this time worked with the deputy commissioner of Darjeeling, A.W. Paul. Finally, in November 1884, after being away for more than four years, he was back in Darjeeling. Sadly for Kinthup, his mother had died while he was away. In the weeks after his return, Kinthup drew no attention. Things changed somewhat when his account found a receptive audience of sorts.

Kinthup Tells His Story

As Kinthup could neither read nor write, he had no written observations of his travels, nor records of any kind. But his recounting of places he had passed, and his descriptions, proved credible and impressed many. It would be another two years before his story was finally documented. Kinthup dictated an account of his travels to Lama Ugyen Gyatso, and it was translated into English. This narrative was then compiled by Colonel Tanner into a report published in 1888 by the Survey of India. The account had a map tracing the Tsangpo's course, all based on information Kinthup had supplied. Kinthup received an award, and a grant of 3,000 rupees.

Though his observations proved invaluable for future generations of explorers and scholars, in his own lifetime, Kinthup's work was given less importance than those of other pandits. He later went on another expedition in a minor capacity, and then resumed much of his old life, as tailor and occasional guide.

9

CYCLING LONG AND CLIMBING HIGH

FANNY BULLOCK WORKMAN IN THE HIMALAYAS

There was no stopping Fanny Workman and her husband, William, as they cycled across India, and then turned their attention to the Himalayas and the Siachen Glacier.

Fanny Bullock Workman was a bit of everything: a cyclist, a mountaineer, an adventurer, a writer and an advocate of women's rights. Born in 1859 in the US, she grew up amid wealth and privilege. Her father was, for a while, the governor of Massachusetts, a state in north-east United States. Her growing-up days were an exciting time when all kinds of progressive ideas were popular. Women were fighting for various social causes like the right to vote, to study at universities that still denied them entry in certain subjects, for issues of dress reform, and to work in professions for long closed to them, such as journalism and medicine.

Two of a Kind

In the 1880s, Fanny Bullock Workman and her husband, William Hunter Workman, moved from the US to Europe. Doctors had suggested that the move would help improve William Workman's health, but it also coincided with the invention of the safety bicycle. This was different from the older penny-farthing bicycle, which had a high front wheel. The safety bicycle had wheels that were same-sized and made of rubber, and a chain pedal system that made riding less dangerous.

In Europe, the Workmans, who were each other's best inspiration, dedicated themselves to travel and exploration. They criss-crossed little-known lands and climbed inaccessible peaks. In 1897, having cycled through Spain and Portugal, and then through parts of North Africa, they began a 14,000-mile (22,530 km) cycling trip from south to north India, and later, they rode from east to west in the subcontinent. Fanny made quite an impression as she rode through the Indian countryside, wearing the ankle-length skirts that she preferred over anything else. They used other kinds of transportation too – boats, trains, bullock carts and the *palki* (palanquin) – and wrote about their adventures.

In 1898, the Workmans put their cycles away and began exploring the mountains, especially the treacherous, inaccessible ranges of the Karakoram to the west of the Himalayas. Between 1899 and 1912, they made as many as six expeditions to the Karakoram mountains and the western Himalayas. A place that was of special fascination to them was the Siachen Glacier. At that time, this was an icy wasteland, in an ill-defined border area. (It remains so even today, but is also a strongly militarized area, with outposts manned and defended by the Indian Army.)

Early Adventures in Europe

Fanny Workman's first climbing experience was in the company of her husband, William. He was a physician educated at Yale and Harvard in the US, and later in Munich, Germany. William and Fanny Workman first ascended the peaks of New Hampshire in north-eastern US. In the late 1880s, they scaled Alpine peaks like the Matterhorn and Mont Blanc in Europe. As they were both such dedicated travellers, Rachel, their daughter, grew up in the care of nannies and in boarding schools. A young son, Siegfried, born in 1893, tragically died as a toddler.

In 1896, their first book, called *Algerian Memories: A Bicycle Tour over the Atlas to the Sahara*, based on their cycling tour of Algeria, was published. This was followed by Fanny's *Sketches Awheel in Modern Iberia*, after they had cycled down Spain and Portugal. Their third book was about their Indian cycling adventures, *Through Town and Jungle – Fourteen Thousand Miles A-wheel Among Temples and People or the Indian Plain*.

Their cycling books as well as their five mountaineering books were all jointly written. They are lively in tone and had entertaining observations – even if this appears somewhat old-fashioned today – of life and people in the places they visited. Before they commenced their travels, they made sure to read English translations of the epics, *Ramayana* and *Mahabharata*, as well as the Buddhist Jataka tales. An admiration of India's ancient culture came almost spontaneously to them.

Cycling Through India

Fanny and William Workman set great faith in their own observations and were very critical of the standard *Murray Guidebooks* popular at the time. Later, they insisted that their first-hand records of mountain surveys confirmed – or negated, as the case could be – the observations of the Trigonometrical Survey of India. They were opinionated in a similar way about a lot of other things: the caste system, the superiority of the brahmins and the behaviour of domestic helpers, among other topics. They felt the Taj Mahal had been overpraised, and that the Chalukyan temples and Ajanta paintings showcased the best of local artisanal abilities. Their account also revealed their travails while looking for accommodation in dak bungalows built for British officials and inns, and the many things found wanting in railway station waiting rooms.

The Nilgiri mountains in the south captured their fancy early. It was aptly named, they wrote, and approaching it was like 'nearing an enchanted land on wings'.

They complained about the overuse of red chillies in food, especially in railway refreshment rooms, which usually served up hurriedly prepared soups and two or three other courses of food: 'A thin smoky soup made from some dried soup stock kept on hand; chicken

FANNY WORKMAN CYCLING IN INDIA

cutlets, pieces of fried chicken with a small bone stuck into each; chicken curry with rice, or roast chicken; and a milk pudding or a custard made with eggs laid by some female relative of the deceased chickens, which served to provide the preceding courses'.

Temples of the South

They admired several of India's historical buildings. When they cycled to the interior of Karnataka, after fording the River Kaveri, they discovered the beauty of the Chalukyan temples at Somanathapura. The friezes, with their intricate carvings, held their complete attention. Some merited a detailed description. One frieze, in particular, enchanted the Workmans. It had a series of

THE FRIEZE PROBABLY DESCRIBED BY FANNY WORKMAN
AND HER HUSBAND

intricately carved elephants in the bottom row; horsemen appeared in the row above; over this, came a scroll interspersed with gargoyles and grotesque lions that were once the royal emblem, followed by a scene from the *Mahabharata*, and finally, a string of geese, regarded as a sacred symbol, appeared right on top. Other panels had rows of gods, including Vishnu in different avatars.

Some of the finest buildings in the city of Bijapur, the capital of a kingdom in the Deccan, were constructed in the reign of Adil Shah II during the seventeenth century. The architects were skilled in designing domes, cornices and brackets. Added to these were the wonderful tracery carvings on windows and screens.

The fresco paintings in the Ajanta caves were preserved well enough to show the perfection of art in those early times. They represented scenes from the Jataka stories about the Buddha's life, and also local events of the time. A beautiful fresco showed the temptation of a meditating Buddha by the demon Mara. In the artistry displayed, and the delicacy of execution, the Workmans noted the close resemblance between the Ajanta frescoes and early Renaissance artists of Italy of the thirteenth and fourteenth centuries.

The Taj Mahal

The Taj Mahal intrigued the Workmans.

They felt the Taj Mahal compared poorly to the domes of buildings in Old Delhi, and the subtle majestic curve of the domes at Gwalior and Mandu. According to them, the Taj's exquisite marble carving had an equal in the tomb of Itimad-ud-daulah in Agra. The Jain temples in Gujarat also displayed superb marble-cut interiors.

Jeypore (or Jaipur) was a 'modern' commercial and manufacturing city lit with gas and with no trace of the sleepiness characteristic of other Indian cities. Its streets were wide but dusty and overcrowded. Jaipur, even then, was known for its 'pink' buildings, which the Workmans described as 'tomato sauce–coloured'.

Jodhpur, on the other hand, was one of the most striking cities on their travels. The city lay at the foot of a steep hill, and an old fort with red walls marked by battlements loomed over it. Massive bastions winded upward and downward in an irregular line along the hill. Seen from a distance, the Workmans wrote, the fort looked like a red rose in the golden desert sands.

Everywhere they went they were amazed at the variety of people they encountered: 'They wore garments of every shade, such as sashes of red and tinsel, turbans of orange, mauve and green, and the bazaars displayed many bright-coloured stuff'. In Sholapur, a town in western India, where the plague then raged, they saw the sea of tents outside the city. This was where the afflicted were housed. Sanitary camps guarded the approaches to infected districts and everyone was subjected to close scrutiny.

The Grandest Road

Like the Taj Mahal, even the Grand Trunk Road had been, the Workmans insisted, overrated. Other cyclists spoke of it as 'the finest cycling track in the world', but the Workmans did not find it quite such a cyclist's

Full of Punctures

Punctures often posed a peril and inconvenience. As the Workmans moved through central and north India, the banyan, mango and tamarind trees of the south were replaced by acacias with thin foliage and an enormous quantity of thorns. Almost every other species of shrub or bush had thorns. These pricked people and bicycles alike, causing pain and innumerable punctures respectively.

paradise, for in places it was worn out and was strewn with loose stones.

Pahalgam in Kashmir was the farthest north they cycled. They travelled to some places by train, and sometimes by boat. Fanny Workman memorably recounted a *palki* ride from Puri to Konark to see the 'Black Pagoda'. The two *palki*s were borne by six bearers, three to each pole. The bearers hummed simple songs, almost in unison. They set a quick pace, reaching the temple at Konark by sunrise. The singing made the journey very pleasant, and the blanket and pillow added to the comfort.

An Unhappy Experience

Their first adventure in the mountains was an attempt to scale the Kanchenjunga in Sikkim. This experience, however, turned out to be an unpleasant one.

A PORTRAIT OF FANNY WORKMAN

Sikkim was then known as the rainiest mountain region in India. The government authorities, moreover, were reluctant to grant the necessary passes and assistance to anyone, especially foreigners like the Workmans, who contemplated investigating the heights bordering the forbidden lands of Nepal and Tibet. The political officer tried to dissuade them, offering several reasons: the density of rhododendron forests beyond Guicha La (pass), the altitude being unsuited for a woman, the general difficulties and slipperiness of the route, and the problems that the rivers posed.

In the end, days into the climb, the Workmans gave up because the porters they hired refused to go ahead and many simply vanished after a day's work. They felt they weren't being paid enough.

Six Times into the Mountains

In 1899, they turned their attention to the Karakoram range, which had only just begun drawing the attention of explorers and surveyors. This vast chain of mountains was to the west of the Himalayas, then in the area made up of present-day Ladakh and Baltistan (an area designated in old survey maps as 'Little Tibet'). It had some of the highest peaks in the world, several being above 18,000 feet; the glaciers were long and challenging.

Over the next 14 years, between 1899 and 1912, the Workmans led six major expeditions in this region and had several interesting adventures. As early as 1899, Fanny set her first altitude record for women by climbing the 21,000-foot high Kosur Gunje. She wrote about it in their book, *In the Ice World of Himalaya: Among the Peaks and Passes of Ladakh, Nubra, Suru, and Baltistan...* (1900).

She completed the ascent soon after a cycling trip in tropical Java, where temperatures had been around mid-40° Celsius. In Java, as she wrote, she had climbed a few dormant volcanoes. She had spent two weeks after that sailing back to India in a steamer, then travelled by train across the heated plains, before finally arriving in Srinagar from Rawalpindi on a *tonga*. She had had no special training in mountain climbing. She described herself as 'not a lightweight and a slow climber', but her powers of endurance stood her in good stead.

Long-Drawn Arrangements

It helped that most times Fanny and William were helped through the most arduous and difficult stretches by their porters who carried them across. The Workmans prepared for their expeditions carefully. At this time, there was very little special mountaineering equipment available. They carried flannel-lined 'mummery tents', and equipped themselves with padded ground sheets, eiderdown-filled sleeping sacks and camel-hair blankets. Sometimes these proved inadequate in the cold, and so they slept in the high mountain base camps with all

ALL SET TO CONQUER MOUNTAINS

their clothing on. There were no tough and lightweight synthetic tents, or ropes, no radios and compact cameras and instruments, and no dehydrated food either. They travelled with cumbersome photography equipment and scientific instruments, screwed steel nails into the sides of their boots to stop slipping on icy slopes and wore heavy tweed clothes to brave the icy winds. Their supplies and outfits were all purchased in Europe and sent to India by ship ahead of their arrival, and then on by railway to Srinagar.

There was the more complex problem of hiring assistants, coolies, porters and helpers. They always hired one or two European guides for their expert knowledge of snow and ice conditions.

Despite the experts, the Workmans made every final decision, deciding their routes in the barren unmapped territory. They made scientific observations and took photos to illustrate their books. They wrote of their expeditions in five books, the last of which described their adventures in the Siachen Glacier, a region they found challenging and utterly fascinating.

Competitive Climbing

In 1903, they first explored the Choga Lungma Glacier in the Gilgit–Baltistan region (in the Karakoram area), and later that summer in June, they explored the Hoh Lumba Glacier, west of the Hispar Glacier, right to its source. During this expedition, William Workman reached an altitude of 23,394 feet, about 300 feet higher than the summit of Aconcagua in the Andes in South America.

The view, he wrote, was a grand one. To the southeast rose the giant peaks of the Biafo, the Mustagh, Masherbrum and Gasherbrum, while the sharp pyramid of Mount K2 towered over all surrounding peaks and ridges. On the south, Haramosh and the immense mass of Nanga Parbat formed a fitting background to other majestic mountains.

The peak and glacier group of the Nun Kun, southwest of Srinagar, was the object of their 1906 expedition. Here, Fanny Workman made her great ascent of the Pinnacle peak that she measured at 23,300 feet. By this achievement, she noted that she had won a place, along with her husband, among the small band of mountaineers who had reached a height of over 23,000 ft.

Lured by unmapped glaciers as well as unconquered peaks, the Workmans devoted their 1908 expedition to exploring the complicated 38-mile (61 km) long Hispar Glacier in the Baltistan region.

Fanny Sticks to Her Guns

They succeeded in crossing the Hispar Pass at around 17,500 feet and descending the 37-mile (59.5 km) long Biafo Glacier. Traversing the two glaciers that were joined at the Hispar Pass constituted a total ice journey of 75 miles (120 km), and this was another record of the time.

As Fanny wrote in the *National Geographic*, this made her the only woman who had made the first ascent of one of the great Himalayan glaciers or any other of equal size. Fanny quite zealously guarded her reputation as a skilled and pioneering mountaineer. When any other woman challenged her altitude record, she was roused to indignation and used all her resources – intellectual and monetary – to prove her opponent wrong. The Workmans had inherited considerable wealth, including land, and this came in handy in financing their travels.

For instance, Annie Peck, another American woman, claimed to have reached a height above 23,000 ft, especially when she ascended Mount Huascaran in Peru in 1908. An outraged Fanny enlisted the aid of French experts who travelled to Peru (at the Workmans' expense) to measure the mountain in question. From their report, Fanny concluded that the altitude that Peck claimed to have attained was some 1,500 feet lower than the highest altitude that Fanny Workman had achieved. It led to a bitter exchange between the two mountaineers.

Fanny succeeded in getting the attention of the male-dominated Royal Geographical Society. In 1905, she became the second woman after Isabella Bird (an English explorer, naturalist, photographer and writer) to make a speech there. But, soon, she had even grander ambitions – to go where no Westerner, especially a woman, had never gone before – Siachen.

The Amazing Rose Glacier

North of Ladakh, in the eastern Karakoram range, the Siachen glacier was once dismissed as a wasteland but is now of strategic and geopolitical significance. The longest glacier in non-polar areas, until the early twentieth century this over 40-mile (64 km) mass of slow-flowing ice was one of the last unexplored gaps on the map. The Workmans explored it twice between 1911 and 1912.

Fanny was intrigued by how the glacier had got its name. As she learnt, Siachen literally meant 'rose-bush': 'Sia' was the Balti name for jungle rose, while 'chen' meant a collection of thorns! Such hardy and wild rosebushes were prevalent in the icy river drains or had taken root in the glacial till, i.e., the sediments borne along by the glacier. The flowers flourished in pink and white splendour on the tongues (or mouths) of several glaciers, especially the Siachen.

She preferred the name, Rose Glacier, to Siachen, pleased by the incongruity of the dainty label when applied to a challenging region of rock and ice.

The Workmans picked the August of 1911 as the best time to journey to Siachen. For a month, they were challenged by poor visibility during the day, variable weather and glacial conditions – the surface was icy and slippery. The Siachen tongue could not be accessed at all before this month owing to the volume of water in the River Nubra that flowed through it, and the alarming presence of quicksand. It rendered traversing the glacier at different fording-points dangerous. Not very many porters could be engaged to travel with them.

They set up base at Goma in the Saltoro valley, west of Siachen and separated from it by the 10-mile (16 km) Ghyari *nullah*. Between the Saltoro and Siachen also lay the 13-mile-(21 km) long and difficult Bilafond Glacier, the 18,400-foot Bilafond La (pass) and then the 7-mile-long (11 km) Lolofond Glacier. All of this presented a difficult approach, but they prevailed, reaching the Siachen at a height of about 16,000 feet.

When they hiked into terra incognita, that is, the area called the Silver Throne plateau of the Siachen Glacier, William snapped an iconic photo of his wife, in a long tweed skirt and ribboned hat, holding up a newspaper article headlined, 'Votes for Women'.

A FAMOUS PHOTOGRAPH OF FANNY WORKMAN IN SIACHEN GLACIER

Led by Fanny, the Workmans were the first to study the full sweep of the region, cataloguing its biological and geological diversity, naming its peaks and valleys – though in many cases, their names were turned down by disgruntled scholars and explorers – and measuring its contours. It was work that confirmed the Siachen as the world's longest glacier beyond the polar regions.

Once More to Siachen

In 1912, their last expedition was made on Fanny's initiative, for the mysterious and challenging Siachen Glacier had lured her back. The Workmans hired a range of experts like Grant Peterkin of the Royal Geographical Society as surveyor and Sarjan Singh from the Survey of India as his assistant. These organizations loaned the

Workmans several important instruments like plane-tables and chronometer watches. Cyprien Savoye, an Italian who had been with the Workmans on previous expeditions, was hired again as were other Italian guides and porters. All had Himalayan and Alpine experience.

One of their Italian porters perished in that expedition, when he fell into a precipice. The expedition was overcome with grief. Garbled reports reached American and British papers that the Workmans had succumbed in the same accident as well.

That year, they made for Baltistan for easier access to Siachen. From Kapalu on the lower River Shyok river they reached Goma, the last base camp in the Saltoro valley. From here, they ascended the Ghyari *nala* once again to reach Siachen. Fanny explored its entire length – 45 miles (72 km) to its source on the watershed between the Indus and Turkestan (Central Asia) basins.

Fanny was dedicated in every sense to the cause of women. In her will, she left a then huge sum of $125,000 to four American women's colleges – Bryn Mawr, Radcliffe, Smith and Wellesley. Her Bryn Mawr bequest, added to by a gift from William, established the Fanny Bullock Workman travelling fellowship. It was awarded for a great many years.

The Workmans retired to the south of France as the First World War broke out. Fanny died in Cannes in 1925 after a long and painful illness. William returned to Massachusetts, and he died at ninety-one, twelve years later.

10

THE SECRETS OF A SWAMP MONSTER

RALPH IZZARD AND THE BURU

The *buru* was the most unusual and strangest of creatures. When stories of the *buru* first emerged, it was described as living in the remotest, least accessible parts of north-east India. It was bluish white in colour and around 15 feet in length. Its skin glistened like that of a fish, though it had no scales. Instead, along its side and back, there were rows of spines. Its triangular head ended in a great snout, flattened at the tip. The *buru* walked on short stumpy legs and defended itself ably with its claws and sharp teeth – especially the large and pointed pair in its upper and lower jaws just like a tiger's or boar's.

A powerful tail, rounded and tapering at the end, gave the *buru* its peculiarly amphibious characteristics, though most often it preferred hiding deep in water. At times though, it was known to raise its neck out of the water and let out a hoarse bellowing cry. It also appeared by the muddy banks of lake swamps, nosing around, swaying its head and neck from side to side.

What the Scientists Said

These descriptions of the *buru* appeared in accounts of anthropologists who lived and conducted research among the ethnic groups of north-east India. Two of them, working independently, such as the Austrian anthropologist Christoph von Furer-Haimendorf, and the British zoologist and agricultural officer, Charles Stonor, noted down stories told to them about this strange creature.

Neither Furer-Haimendorf, nor Stonor, nor James Mills, his friend, had ever seen the *buru*, nor had they ever heard its harsh bellowing call. The *buru* was part of the lore and figured in several hand-me-down stories narrated to them by older members of the Apatani tribe, who lived in settlements in prsent-day Arunachal Pradesh's Lower Subansiri district. Another Englishman, Ralph Izzard, a British newspaperman then living in Delhi, quite far away from Arunachal Pradesh, read of these accounts and was entranced. He was curious to know more about the *buru*.

RALPH IZZARD

This region of north-east India, made up of river valleys, in parts swampy and marshy, and ringed by high mountains, was then part of Upper Assam. When Furer-Haimendorf was carrying out his research, it was the mid-1940s and the Second World War had just ended. Barely 400 kilometres to the south from Ziro, the main town in Lower Subansiri district, lie Kohima in Nagaland and Imphal in Manipal. These towns saw bitter fighting between British Indian forces and the Japanese between March and July 1944.

Enter the Apatanis

This area, close to the lower Himalayas, and to China and Burma as well, had drawn geologists, botanists and even anthropologists, curious to study the region and societies that lived here. Their studies, in turn, helped ruling governments, who were keen to ensure that border regions located faraway remained secure against enemies.

The stories about the *buru* had their beginnings centuries ago when the Apatanis trekked in groups from the north and east, through the passes of the Himalayas, to settle in this region. In these oral stories, this area was then part of a big swampy lake amid high mountains and drained by numerous rivers. The silt made the area fertile and it was ideal for the Apatanis who chose to settle down as agriculturists.

In the stories Furer-Haimendorf collected by talking to village elders and chiefs, the Apatanis or simply the Tani, fought the *buru* and established their own settlements by clearing the swamps, flooding the fields and beginning the cultivation of rice. It gave their beginnings a heroic touch and their fight with the *buru* put them in a somewhat 'superior' position to other rival ethnic groups in the region.

The Apatani agricultural and settled way of life was different from that of other ethnic groups around them, such as the Miris and the Nishis, who lived by hunting and 'shifting' cultivation. These groups were often in conflict, sometimes bitter and hostile, with the Apatanis. Over the centuries, the agricultural traditions of the Apatani, their knowledge of and familiarity with the landscape made for a thriving cultivation of paddy. (More recently, the UNESCO World Heritage Convention has before it a proposal to include the sustainable traditions and knowledge systems of the Apatanis on the prestigious World Heritage List.)

In these early stories, from the days of long ago, when the Apatanis worked to clear the lakes to make the land suitable to grow paddy, they came across a big and mysterious enemy: the *buru*, whose amphibious nature helped it hide away in the waters.

The *burus* could be dangerous adversaries. According to one story, a hunter who had once killed a young *buru* was in turn killed by its angry mother, who chased him and with one swipe of her immense tail forced him into the swamp where he drowned. In another story, a young woman while drawing water from a stream was scared by a *buru*. When the villagers were told, they dammed up the small stream with the help of boulders and clay, and the *buru* perished.

The ancient Apatani warriors were brave. They had the help of 'magical' brass plates or shields in their fight against the *buru*. A couple of these shields were, it is said, in the keeping of some Apatani families and cherished as heirlooms. This bravery, as Furer-Haimendorf noted, helped them many a time in driving away other groups they came in conflict with.

All these *buru* stories were reconfirmed by Charles Stonor, who visited this region in the late 1940s. Stonor accompanied a government official called James Philip Mills, who had served for long years in this region. Stonor's account got the attention of Ralph Izzard, an adventure-seeking newspaperman.

The Original James Bond

Ralph William Burdick Izzard was born in England in 1910. He had been a journalist with the *Daily Mail* ever since he had graduated from Cambridge University in 1931. He had reported from far-off places like Kenya, Korea, Algeria and Egypt, and had also worked for British intelligence services during the Second World War.

Izzard's rather daring life as a reporter made him worry frequently about there being nothing left to explore any more. He fretted about mysteries dying out and was always on the lookout for strange new stories, especially the kind that had him risking everything to tramp down to remote places. His wife, Molly, whose father had worked in India and who had studied for some years in a boarding school in Darjeeling, shared his interests.

Izzard had actually doubled up a secret service agent on many an occasion; he worked for the British MI5. In 1936, during the time the Nazis rose to power in Germany, Izzard was in Berlin, working for the *Daily Mail*, when German soldiers looking for spies and reporters critical of the regime surrounded the restaurant he was in. A helpful waitress, charmed by Izzard, stowed him away in the bathroom. Confined in that narrow space, Izzard considered flushing his passport down to avoid detection and likely imprisonment. But the soldiers, fobbed off by the insistent restaurant staff – they had many foreign journalists as customers – soon called off their search and dispersed.

Izzard always came up with offbeat ideas. During his time in the British Secret Service as the war raged, Izzard had a plan to 'capture' one of the Nazi encryption machines called the Enigma. It was used to devise secret codes to send messages to the army. Izzard thought of deliberately crashing a captured German bomber on the French coast, then under Nazi control. Then, 'rescued' British soldiers disguised in the uniform of the Luftwaffe – the German Air Force – would infiltrate the Nazi secret service to gather useful information.

Before Izzard could put his 'Operation Ruthless' into operation, British forces managed to capture a German U-boat (a submarine), and an Enigma machine was soon in British hands. In Buenos Aires in Argentina, Izzard's boss in the British Secret Service, Sir Ian Fleming, watched him playing poker with Nazi officers. Fearless, Izzard wasn't in the least bothered by the odds he was playing against. All this was soon after the war, when some Nazis, trying to evade capture for their gruesome crimes, were on the run. Many had fled to friendly South American nations. This scene inspired Sir Ian Fleming and was immortalized in the first James Bond book he wrote, *Casino Royale*.

Izzard Learns of the Buru

Soon after this, Izzard found himself in India. The Second World War had ended, and in India's north-east, Assam had played an important role. Here, the British (whose army was largely Indian) and Allied forces had set up a base to counter the Japanese advance. While this region was in the news, with battles in Kohima and Imphal, there were large parts still unexplored.

Stationed in Delhi, Izzard reported for the *Daily Mail* on the trauma of Partition that followed India's independence in 1947. But he soon heard about the *buru* from a forest official called Hamilton then on a visit to Delhi. Soon after, Izzard exchanged letters with Charles Stonor. The *buru* stories reminded him of stories by Arthur Conan Doyle and H.G. Wells. They had written about prehistoric creatures such as giant lizards, who lived on in the tropical regions even centuries after their presumed extinction.

Stonor admitted he had not seen the creature, but his curiosity, like Izzard's, had been aroused by all the stories about it. All he did write in his reply to Izzard was that if *buru*s indeed existed, they were reptiles 'the size of an ox, with a prominent snout'. Stonor surmised that the *buru* was either a crocodile ancestor or a dinosaur.

Stonor pointed to two actual sites related to the *buru* stories. One area the Apatani had pointed out to him had the 'burial sites' of the *buru*, and in another, fifty miles (80 km) further to the north-east, the *buru* was rumoured to have been sighted. No one ever knew who had seen it; it was always someone who knew someone else who had heard the story.

Like-Minded Friends

Such stories about the *buru* were also part of cryptozoology, considered a 'pseudoscience' (a set of theories or beliefs some people claim are based on scientific fact, even though in reality they they may not be). This subject had quite a following among those fascinated by animals rumoured to be in existence but never really seen. Izzard had been interested in the subject since his schooldays.

Two of his friends from college days, Ivan Terrance Sanderson and Gerald Russell, were also deeply interested in cryptozoology. Sanderson had been on expeditions to some of the world's most remote places, including dense jungles and forbidding valleys, trying to collect interesting tales of animals believed to be 'lost'. He wrote books on natural history that were popular between the 1930s and 1950s. These include *Animal Treasure* (1937), *Caribbean Treasure* (1939), *Animal Tales* (1946), *Follow the Whale* (1956) and *Monkey Kingdom* (1957), among others. He also wrote for the *Saturday Evening Post* on strange mysterious creatures like sea monsters and dinosaurs.

In 1961, Sanderson wrote a book on the mysterious creature in the Himalayas, which came to be known as the Abominable Snowman and went by other names like the Yeti or Bigfoot. It was described as a giant hairy hominoid. Sanderson remained a close friend of Izzard's, advising the latter as he searched for cryptids (animals living in secret) like the Yeti, and later the *buru*.

Gerald Russell too was an explorer in his own right. In 1932, he went to Africa, where in British Cameroon (now part of Nigeria in West Africa), he described meeting a strange unknown animal called 'Mokele Mbembe' – meaning a creature that 'stops a river flowing'– an elephant-sized amphibious creature, with a long neck, and a tail that could stay submerged in the water for a long time. It was supposed to be an herbivore, but its terrifying roar scared away both humans and animals.

Later, Russell also went on an expedition to look for the *beisung* or giant panda in China. During 1936–37, he played a part in capturing the first giant panda: a half-grown tame one wandering on a farm and thriving on grass and other vegetation. In the early 1940s, Russell travelled to China again to capture a rare little-known animal, the golden takin – a goat antelope that is today an endangered species – but as the Chinese Communist Party advanced during that country's civil war, he was forced to quickly abandon his expedition.

Buru Burial Sites

When Stonor and Mills visited the Apatanis in the mid-1940s, they listened to legends about how the *buru* had been vanquished. The Apatanis even showed them the exact spots at which four *burus* were said to have been killed and buried in the long ago past.

THE BURU: ARTIST'S IMPRESSION

From these stories, they tried to come up with a picture of the *buru*. Something like Furer-Haimendorf's description but clearly different. The *buru*, they wrote, was a kind of quasi-prehistoric 'saurian'. They even considered the possibility that the Apatanis had heard descriptions of the crocodile or the gharial that thrived in the River Ganga. These stories had gathered exaggerated details over generations. The fact that a *buru* knocked a man into the water with its tail, to Stonor, suggested a similarity with a crocodile that lived in the Sunderbans. It could even be compared to the monitor lizard or Komodo dragon of South-East Asia.

All these *buru* stories simply fascinated Izzard. Though there was nothing definitive, for a *buru* – real, dead, or even buried – had never been sighted, he convinced his newspaper, *The Daily Mail*, to finance the expedition. Later, he even wrote a book that described every theory related to the *buru* and his own wild-goose chase trying to track one down.

Izzard Makes Plans

In 1950, Izzard, accompanied by Stonor, travelled to upper Assam (now part of Arunachal Pradesh), determined to traverse the old Apatani trails in search of the *buru*. They set up a team of porters, along with collapsible boats, and organized gifts for the headmen and chiefs of the various ethnic groups they would meet. They hacked their way through the forests, endured heavy rain, and suffered the endless bites of leeches and mosquitoes. The swamps were downright dangerous and they had to watch every step. Izzard described all this in his book, written in 1951, called *Hunt for the Buru: The True Story of the Search for a Prehistroic Reptile in North India.*

Yet, for all his efforts, Izzard never caught sight of the *buru*. Finally, after a few months, he consoled himself with the fact that it was winter, the time the *buru*s hibernated in the high mountain caves all around the valley. Izzard, who badly wanted to sight a 'live buru' wrote of glimpsing at times the strange shadows on the surface of the lake, but these were just assumptions, and really came to nothing. The lake, the rumoured home of the burus, was far too shallow to conceal anything.

Izzard Has Other Adventures

Despite this, Izzard's thirst for adventure remained unquenched. Two years later, as Sir John Hunt prepared for his famous expedition to Mount Everest, Izzard was determined to get a 'scoop' for his newspaper, though *The Times* (London) had already secured the rights to report on the expedition. It was in Kathmandu's British Embassy that Hunt and his team camped first, meeting reporters and hosting press conferences. Izzard did manage an interview with Tenzing Norgay, who complained of the poor facilities the Sherpas received, though they did most of the gruelling work on expeditions. A furious John Hunt declared Izzard an 'enemy of the expedition' and refused to share any information with him.

An undaunted Izzard set out on his own, without

compass or map, to work out the route taken by Hunt as he headed for the Everest. Izzard took a week to walk from Kathmandu to Tengboche, and in another three days, he had located the Everest base camp. One of Hunt's colleagues wrote later of how Izzard, despite the freezing temperatures, was smartly dressed in a sports jacket though his lips had turned blue and his eyes were inflamed in a clear case of snow-blindness. Some months later, Izzard would leave for another adventure with his friend, Gerald Russell. This time as well, he failed to find the 'yeti', but he did manage to write another book, *The Abominable Snowman Adventure*.

Other Swamp Monsters

People who study origin myths believe that 'lacustrine' or lake-dwelling, monsters, are familiar to several groups of mountain peoples. For instance, there is said to be a monster of some sort in a reputedly bottomless pool near Viswema village in the Angami Naga country that makes people afraid to bathe in it. The Pala Lake in Lakher country of Myanmar issued from a hole where a monstrous snake once lived. Mythical creatures similar to the *burus* also appear in stories from Iran, that talk of the dragon called *ahi*. The ancient Vedas also record that the *asura* Vritra was known as Ahi. As a dragon, he held the waters captive and caused a drought before he was killed by Indra.

Ralph Izzard, never tiring of excitement, next took on assignments in West Asia. With his wife, Molly, he wrote a book based on their long years in Lebanon, where he had first-hand glimpse of conflicts in Cyprus, Egypt and Palestine. Another book, *Smelling the Breezes*, tells of the 300-mile (483 km) expedition of the Izzard family – including their two sons and two daughters, between the ages of nine and four – across the hills of Lebanon in 1957. It was a journey on three donkeys with their cook doubling up as interpreter, and they had a delightful summer holiday. Izzard was clearly a man for all seasons, always up for adventure of every kind.

ACKNOWLEDGEMENTS

History is complex and increasingly, more contested. I try in my own way to make it entertaining and interesting for the young reader. I especially want them to think things out for themselves, to realize that the past is always with us and in how we see the present and the future. I've learnt from all those who taught me, unhesitatingly and ungrudgingly, and I'd really like to thank them for everything they have helped me with.

Vatsala Kaul Banerjee and everyone at Hachette India over the years.

My parents, Uma and Chinmay Chakrabarty. Krishna Raj and Maithreyi Krishnaraj. Subba Rao, the late Narayan Dutt*ji*, Luis Fernandes, Jayanthi Mahalingam, and Meera Nair at Amrita Bharati, Mumbai.

My teachers over the years, and there are some whose first names I never knew, sadly: Mrs Peri Shastri at school, Nina Burman, Sangeeta Luthra Sharma, Neeru Ailavadi, Neena Gupta, Archana Sahai, Meera Baijal, Kamala Gupta, Debarati Bhattacharji, Gyan Pandey, Sumit Sarkar, Madhukar Shukla, Geeta Saxena and Mariam Dossal.

My friends at the *EPW*: Padma Prakash, Gauraang, Leela, James, Nutan, Deepali, and Lina Mathias.

Ram Reddy at *The India Forum*, and Naresh Fernandes and Aman Khanna at *Scroll*.

Friends like Moazzam Sheikh, Dipankar Das, Shruti Pandey and Arpita Das, who always appreciated my love for history.

And of course, for their support, always, in spite of everything, Ajay and Devyani.

FURTHER READING

Most of the following books are in the public domain and available on archive.org:

Alder, Garry. *Beyond Bokhara: The Life of William Moorcroft, Asian Explorer and Veterinary Surgeon, 1767–1825*. London: Century, 1985.

Bhattacharya, Parimal. *Bells of Shangri-La: Scholars, Spies and Invaders in Tibet*. Gurugram: HarperCollins India, 2019.

———, and Sarat Chandra Das. *Journey to Lhasa, the Diary of a Spy*. New Delhi: Speaking Tiger Books, 2017.

Burnes, Alexander. *Travels into Bokhara. Being an account of a Journey from India to Cabool, Tartary and Persia. Also, narrative of a Voyage on the Indus from the Sea to Lahore*. Vol. 1, 1st ed. London: John Murray, 1834.

Das, Sarat Chandra. Journey to Lhasa & Central Tibet. 1st ed., London: John Murray, 1902. Republished as *Lhasa and Central Tibet*. New Delhi: Cosmo Publications, 2003. First edition accessed on archive.org.

———. *Indian Pandits in the Land of Snow*. Reprint, New Delhi: Rupa, 2006. First published 1893 by Baptist Mission Press (Calcutta).

Grant, Colesworthy. *Rough Pencillings of a Rough Trip to Rangoon in 1846*. Calcutta: Thacker, Spink & Co., 1853. Accessed on archive.org.

———. *Anglo-Indian Domestic Life: A Letter from an Artist in India to His Mother in England. Subarnarekha*. Calcutta: Thacker, Spink & Co., 1862. Accessed on archive.org.

Gupta, Hari Ram. *Life and Work of Mohan Lal Kashmiri, 1812–1877*, 1st ed. Lahore: Minerva Book Shop, 1943.

Hooker, Joseph Dalton. *Himalayan journals; or, Notes of a Naturalist in Bengal, the Sikkim and Nepal Himalayas, the Khasia Mountains.* 2 vols. London: John Murray, 1854.

Izzard, Ralph. *The Hunt for the Buru.* Fresno, California: Craven Street Books, 2001. First published 1951 by Hodder and Stoughton (London).

Lal, Mohan, *Journal of a tour through the Punjab, Afghanistan, Turkistan, Khorasan and Part of Persia in Company with Lt Burnes, and Dr Gerard.* Calcutta: Baptist Mission Press, 1934. Accessed from archive.org.

———. *Travels in the Panjab, Afghanistan, & Turkistan, to Balk, Bokhara, and Herat; and a visit to Great Britain and Germany.* Reprinted, Lahore: Al Biruni, 1979. First published 1846 by W.H. Allen & Co. (Calcutta).

Markham, Clements. *Travels in Peru and India.* London: John Murray, 1862.

Moorcroft, William, and George Trebeck. *Travels in the Himalayan Provinces of Hindustan and the Panjab; in Ladakh and Kashmir; in Peshawar, Kabul, Kunduz, and Bokhara, from 1819–1825.* Vol.1 and Vol. 2, edited by Horace Hayman Wilson. London: John Murray, 1841.

Montgomerie, T. G. (1868a). "Report of a Route-Survey Made by Pundit, from Nepal to Lhasa, and Thence Through the Upper Valley of the Brahmaputra to Its Source." *The Journal of the Royal Geographical Society of London* 38: 129–219.

Stewart, Jules. Spying for the Raj: The Pundits and the Mapping of the Himalaya. Cheltenham: History Press, 2006.

Waller, Derek. *The Pundits: British Exploration of Tibet and Central Asia.* Lexington: University Press of Kentucky, 2004.

Workman, Fanny and William Workman. *In the Ice World of Himálaya, Among the Peaks and Passes of Ladakh, Nubra, Suru, and Baltistan.* New York: Cassell & Company Limited, 1900. p. 204.

———. *Ice-Bound Heights of the Mustagh: An Account of Two Seasons of Pioneer Exploration and High Climbing in the Baltistan Himalaya.* London: A. Constable & Co., 1908. p. 444.

———. *Peaks and Glaciers of Nun Kun: A Record of Pioneer-Exploration and Mountaineering in the Punjab Himalaya.* London: A. Constable & Co. Ltd., 1909. p. 411.

———. *The Call of the Snowy Hispar: A Narrative of Exploration and Mountaineering on the Northern Frontier of India.* New York: Scribner, 1911. p. 520.

———. *Two Summers in the Ice-Wilds of Eastern Karakoram: The Exploration of Nineteen Hundred Square Miles of Mountain and Glacier.* New York: E. P. Dutton & Company, 1916. p. 578.

IMAGE COPYRIGHT INFORMATION

All images are sourced from Wikimedia Commons Public Domain except where mentioned otherwise.

PRELIMS: Pages i and vi: Chinmayee Samant

CHAPTER 1: The World's Fastest Horse: Page 3: By kind courtesy of: RCVS (Royal College of Veterinary Surgeons) Knowledge; **Pages 10–11:** 'Approach to Yarkand', 1868, from the 1871 book, *Visits to High Tatary*; Author: Robert B. Shaw; **Page 13:** Online gallery of the British Library, 1844; Author: Eden, Emily; Cropped **Pages 14–15:** Xinjiang Quan Tu (Atlas of Xinjiang). Chart 15 - Yarkand. This map is available from the United States Library of Congress's Geography & Map Division under the digital ID g7823xm. gct00164; Author: Unknown; **Page 19:** English: V0050528 Credit: Wellcome Library, London; Author: James Rattray; **Pages 22–23:** Turkoman Horse, 1848; Author: F. Joseph Cardini

CHAPTER 2: Many Disguises, Many Lands: Page 27: Mohan Lal Kashmiri: Unknown author; **Page 28:** Portrait of Alexander Burnes; British Museum, London: https://www.britishmuseum.org/collection/object/P_1970-0527-2-2; © The Trustees of the British Museum, released as CC BY-NC-SA 4.0; **Page 31:** Maharaja Ranjit Singh on horseback with attendants with all dressed in Basant (yellow), 19th century; Author: Unknown; Source: https://www.reddit.com/r/Sikh/comments/lmauz0/basant_panchmi_kanhaiya_lals_tarikelahore_1884/; **Page 32:** Sultan Mohammad Khan; watercolour by a Company artist, Punjab, ca.1865; National Army Museum; Author: Unknown; Indian company artist; Converted to black-and-white; **Page 33:** Buddhas of Bamiyan, from: Iwan Lawrowitsch Jaworski: Reise der russischen Gesandtschaft in Afghanistan und Buchara in den Jahren 1878-79, Jena : Costenoble, 1885; Source: http://www.bassenge.com/; Unknown author; **Page 38:** A Portrait of the Crown Prince, Abbas Mirza; Christie's London, South Kensington Saleroom, Author: L. Herr; **Page 39:** Dost Mohammad Khan, 1793 to 1863. Emir of Afghanistan. From The World's Inhabitants by G.T. Bettany published 1888; Author: Bettany, G. T. (George Thomas)

CHAPTER 3: In the Land of Golden Pagodas: Page 44: Colesworthy Grant: Source: The Life of Colesworthy Grant by Peary Chand Mittra, 1881; **Page 48:** Ann Judson: Portrait from the Welsh Portrait Collection at the National Library of Wales; Artist: Richard Woodman, c. 1826; Converted to black-and-white; **Page 52:** Watercolour with pen and ink of a portrait of Ameegalay, Taline Lady, 1855; Source: Series of Views in Burmah taken during Major Phayre's Mission to the Court of Ava in 1855; Converted to black-and-white; **Page 54:** Watercolour with pen and ink of a view of the King's Palace at Amarapura; Source: 'A Series of Views in Burmah taken during Major Phayre's Mission to the Court of Ava in 1855' by Colesworthy Grant; http://www.bl.uk/onlinegallery/onlineex/apac/other/019wdz000000540u00043000.html; Converted to black-and-white; **Page 56:** Watercolour in pen and ink of the long wooden Bridge crossing the Lake Taungthaman. Source: 'A Series of Views in Burmah taken during Major Phayre's Mission to the Court of Ava in 1855' by Colesworthy Grant; Converted to black-and-white; **Page 59:** Watercolour with pen and ink of the 'Lord White Elephant'; Source: 'A Series of Views in Burmah taken during Major Phayre's Mission to the Court of Ava in 1855' by Colesworthy Grant; Converted to black-and-white

CHAPTER 4: Flower Spotter in the High Hills: Page 62: Source: Christie's; Author: William E. Kiburn; **Page 64: picture 1:** https://archive.org/stream/botanyofantarcti01hook#page/n8/mode/1up; Author: Joseph Dalton Hooker; **picture 2:** Illustration of *Nitophyllum smithi* in Flora Antarctica. Drawn and engraved by Walter Hood Fitch; **picture 3:** Walter Hood Fitch - https://archive.org/details/botanyofantarcti0144hook; Converted to black-and-white; all three from The Botany of the Antarctic voyage of H.M. Discovery Ships

Erebus and *Terror* in the years 1839–43, under the command of Captain Sir James Clark Ross; Author: Hooker, Joseph Dalton, Sir; Artist: Fitch, W. H. (Walter Hood); **Page 65:** Antarctica: image on page 313 of File:A Voyage of Discovery and Research in the Southern and Antarctic Regions Vol. 1.djvu, 1847; Source: https://archive.org/details/voyageofdiscove01ross; **Page 71:** Original source in private collection – copy at http://image.invaluable.com/housePhotos/christies/26/109726/H0027-L03264103.jpg; Author: William Walker after Frank Stone; Converted to black-and-white; **Page 73:** *Rhododendron dalhousiae*: Curtis's botanical magazine 79: 4718. 1853; Author: W.J. Hooker; **Page 74:** *Rhododendron argenteum:* From *The Rhododendrons of the Sikkim-Himalaya* by Joseph Dalton Hooker and illustrated by Walter Hood Fitch; **Page 76:** Tibet and Cholamoo Lake from the summit of the Donkia Pass, looking North West. Originally from *Himalayan Journals*: or, *Notes of a Naturalist in Bengal, the Sikkim and Nepal Himalayas, the Khasia Mountains, Etc.* by Joseph Dalton Hooker

CHAPTER 5: The Search for a Magical Plant: Pages 82, 83, 93, 96–97: Scanned and cropped from *Albert H Markham: The Life of Sir Clements R. Markham*, John Murray, London 1917; Artist: Unknown; Converted to black-and-white; **Page 88:** 1897, Source: List of Koehler Images; Author: Franz Eugen Köhler, Köhler's Medizinal-Pflanzen

CHAPTER 6: Travels to the Forbidden City: Page 102: Nain Singh: http://www.pbs.org/wgbh/pages/frontline/shows/tibet/ascend/singh.html; **Pages 108–109**: Nain's Singh's route map, 1877; Source: https://catalog.princeton.edu/catalog/7122656; **Pages 116–117:** Map of Lhasa, 19th century; Source: Unknown; Author: Hyacinth (1777–1853); Converted to black-and-white

CHAPTER 7: A Headmaster's Secret Journeys: Page 124: Sarat Chandra Das, c. 1895; Source: http://mirknig.com/uploads/posts/2011-02/1297575737_sarat-chandra-das.-puteshestvie-v-tibet.-spb._page011.jpg [1]; Author: S.C. Sen/ Royal Geographical Society; **Page 134:** Map of Lhasa in the beginning of 20th century, 1932; Source: Book Zeměpis světa, díl osmý, Přední Asie a Vysoká Asie. Published by publishing house Aventinum in Prague; Author: Unknown; **Page 136:** Author: Das, Sarat Chandra; Graham Sandberg,

1852–1905; Augutus William Hyde, d. 1907; Title: *A Tibetan-English Dictionary with Sanskrit Synonyms*; Publisher: Calcutta: Bengal Secretariat Book Depot; Publication date: 1902

CHAPTER 8: The Mysteries of a River: Page 145: Kinthup, surveyor for the GTS, 1914; Source: Bailey, F.M. (1914). 'Exploration on the Tsangpo or Upper Brahmaputra', *The Geographical Journal*; Author: Unknown; **Pages 150–151:** Detail from the map (BL Add.Or.3016, f.; 3),https://blogs.bl.uk/asian-and-african/2016/07/the-wise-collection-acquiring-knowledge-on-tibet-in-the-late-1850s.html; Author: British Library blogs; Collector: Thomas Alexander Wise (1802-1889); Converted to black-and-white

CHAPTER 9: Cycling Long and Climbing High: Page 158: Fanny Bullock Workman on her bicycle tour of India, c. 1897; Source: *Through Town and Jungle: Fourteen Thousand Miles A-Wheel Among the Temples and People of the Indian Plain*. London: Unwin, 1904; Author: William Hunter Workman; **Page 159:** Wikimedia Commons Creative CCA-SA 4.0 International license: Chennakesava Temple Sculpture detail (3924883715).jpg; Author: Sarah Welch; Converted to black-and-white and text on image cropped on right side; **Page 163:** Source: This image is available from the United States Library of Congress Prints and Photographs Division under the digital ID cph.3c18944; **Page 165:** US-Public Domain: This image is available from the United States Library of Congress's Prints and Photographs division under the digital ID cph.3b17932; **Page 170:** US-PD; *Two summers in the ice-wilds of eastern Karakoram. The exploration of nineteen hundred square miles of mountain and glacier* by Fanny Bullock Workman and William Hunter Workman with three maps and one hundred and forty-one illustrations by the authors. New York: E.P. Dutton & Company, [1917]

Chapter 10: The Secrets of a Swamp Monster: Page 173: Lt. Commander Ralph Izzard, RNVR (c. 1944); Source: S. Izzard; Author: M. Fitzpatrick, (Izzard); https://commons.wikimedia.org/wiki/File:RalphIzzard.jpg; **Page 181:** Chinmayee Samant